D1045657

"Brian has a great understanding of the social web and financial markets' intersection. I was inspired by Twitter in 2008 and started StockTwits. Learning how to use modern social tools to speed up your knowledge and abilities is something this book will help you accomplish."
—Howard Lindzon, Cofounder of StockTwits

"You have an excellent guide on your journey with the author of this book, Brian Egger. His ability to think clearly about the complex world of investing is first-rate. You are in good hands here."
—Nicholas Colas, Market Strategist

"Brian Egger has successfully defined himself as a leading contributor to the evolving field of the intersection of social media and investment expertise . . . a highly ranked sell-side analyst . . . and author who brings a unique perspective and experiences to the endeavor. Brian's intellect, awareness, and communication skills will allow him to make a mark on investment and finance for many years to come."
—Michael J. Driscoll, EdD, Clinical Professor and Senior Executive-in-Residence, Robert B. Willumstad School of Business, Adelphi University

"Brian Egger brings a unique combination of experience as a highly regarded sell-side analyst, and the knowledge of technology to understanding the changing dynamic of investing. His thoughts and insights into how social media impacts stock price movements will help individual investors play by the 'new set of rules' in investing. A 'must read' for those wanting to stay on top of factors shaping a new paradigm in investing."
—Al Jackson, Managing Member, Siridean Advisors LLC, Former Head of Global Securities Research at Credit Suisse

"Brian's background gives him an exceptional vantage point, which allows him to understand and educate others about the changing landscape of social media, and its significant impact on the world of investing and trading. His book is a great resource during a revolutionary time in the unique history of finance, news, and technology."
—Mark Dimont, Former Director of Business Development at Dataminr

Foreword by **Nicholas Colas**
Chief Market Strategist at ConvergEx Group

SOCIAL MEDIA
STRATEGIES FOR
INVESTING

How **Twitter and Crowdsourcing Tools** Can Make You a Smarter Investor

BRIAN D. EGGER
Wall Street Journal "Best on the Street" Analyst

Adams media
AVON, MASSACHUSETTS

Published by
Adams Media, a division of F+W Media, Inc.
57 Littlefield Street, Avon, MA 02322. U.S.A.
www.adamsmedia.com

ISBN 10: 1-4405-8058-8
ISBN 13: 978-1-4405-8058-1
eISBN 10: 1-4405-8059-6
eISBN 13: 978-1-4405-8059-8

Printed in the United States of America.

10   9   8   7   6   5   4   3   2   1

Library of Congress Cataloging-in-Publication Data

Egger, Brian D.
  Social media strategies for investing / Brian D. Egger, Wall Street Journal, Best on
the Street Analyst; foreword by Nicholas Colas, Chief Market Strategist at ConvergEx.
     pages cm
  Includes bibliographical references and index.
   ISBN 978-1-4405-8058-1 (pb) -- ISBN 1-4405-8058-8 (pb) -- ISBN 978-1-4405-
8059-8 (ebook) -- ISBN 1-4405-8059-6 (ebook)
1. Investments--Computer network resources. 2. Social media. 3. Investment analysis. I. Title.
   HG4515.95.E34 2014
   332.6--dc23
                              2014026411

Many of the designations used by manufacturers and sellers to distinguish their product are claimed as trademarks. Where those designations appear in this book and F+W
Media, Inc. was aware of a trademark claim, the designations have been printed with
initial capital letters.

This publication is designed to provide accurate and authoritative information with
regard to the subject matter covered. It is sold with the understanding that the publisher is not engaged in rendering legal, accounting, or other professional advice. If legal
advice or other expert assistance is required, the services of a competent professional
person should be sought.
—From a *Declaration of Principles* jointly adopted by a Committee of the American Bar
Association and a Committee of Publishers and Associations

Cover design by Jessica Pooler.

This book is available at quantity discounts for bulk purchases.
For information, please call 1-800-289-0963.

Contents

Acknowledgments

Writing *Social Media Strategies for Investing* took me on a year-long journey marked with surprises and detours. I am grateful for the generosity of a number of individuals who helped breathe life into this project and transformed it from an idea into a complete written work. This book would not have become a reality without the advice and input of friends, colleagues, and family.

As a first-time book author, I was fortunate to have in my corner several energetic and passionate individuals who helped me connect with my audience. I extend a special thanks to my literary agent, Linda Konner, for her commitment to the book and her conviction about its potential. My editor, Tom Hardej, provided guidance as I completed the manuscript. His enthusiasm and feedback have been invaluable. I am also grateful to Peter Archer for his fine editing input.

Social finance exists because of the innovative work of entrepreneurs who had the foresight to understand how social media is transforming stock analysis. Several industry leaders articulated their visions and strategy. Howard Lindzon, the cofounder of StockTwits, and Howard's colleague, Sean McLaughlin, provided insights and introductions. I was able to meet with other knowledgeable executives, including Leigh Drogen, the CEO of Estimize; David Greenfield, the Director of Financial Sales at Gnip; Druce Vertes, the founder of StreetEYE; Mark Dimont, the former head of Business Development at Dataminr; Gautham Sastri, the CEO of iSENTIUM; and Jeff Dorman, the Vice President of Business Development at Harvest Exchange. David Jackson, the CEO of *Seeking Alpha*, took time to read part of the manuscript. Yoni Assia, the CEO of eToro, explained to me important aspects of social trading.

A number of experienced financial professionals shared examples of how using social media has informed their investment process. Nick Colas, the Chief Market Strategist at ConvergEx Group, provided suggestions and wrote a wonderful foreword. Joseph Tranfo and Michael Bigger described their experiences on StockTwits, where Michael's influential written work on Plug Power, Inc. has gained a wide following. My former colleague, Ray Deacon, was kind enough to share his observations about the importance of industry blogs. Mark Fane and Jan Urbahn expounded on the merits of listening to investment-related podcasts.

Professor Michael Driscoll introduced me to the faculty and students of Adelphi University, where I gave a well-received lecture on social finance. Dennis Forst described his experiences on the Harvest Exchange, while Mathis Conner explained some lesser-known applications of Google. Josh Brown, the CEO of Ritholtz Wealth Management, provided inspiration for the chapter about investment blogs and imparted some useful thoughts about the growing influence of StockTwits.

One of the challenges of writing *Social Media Strategies for Investing* was managing the BreakingCall (*www.breakingcall.com*) website while devoting much of my time to research and writing. My colleagues at BreakingCall, Michael Anderegg and Nitiin A. Khandkar, lent their support to this book project and kept the wheels turning behind the scenes.

None of what I have accomplished would have been possible without the love and encouragement of my amazing family. I am thankful for the devotion of my beautiful wife, Felicia; my beautiful boys, Brandon and Daniel; my wonderful parents, Nina and Alan; and my dear sister, Amy. I also appreciate the support of our "Canadian family" in Montreal—Judy, Eddie, Robbie, and Ilana—who used social media to spread the word about my book in Canada. I owe my whole family many thanks.

Foreword

Imagine that a wealthy and elderly uncle invites you for a visit. Over lunch, he reveals that he plans to leave you a considerable sum of money in his will. There is a catch, however. He will either leave you $1 million, or you can flip a coin with him. If you win the toss, you get $3 million. If you lose, you get nothing. Your elderly relative has developed a playful streak in his old age!

If you are like most people, you would choose the $1 million "sure thing." But consider the other option for a moment: It is actually worth much more than $1 million because a 50/50 shot at $3 million is "worth" $1.5 million. Still, that $1 million "bird in the hand" would set you up for life. Thanking your uncle for his generosity, you part ways, happy that your financial future is finally secure. His coin, meanwhile, stays safely in his pocket. Imagine the regret you would feel, if you were to lose the coin toss and walk away with nothing.

This story, anchored in the Nobel Prize–winning concept of "prospect theory," reflects an important lesson about how humans make financial decisions: It's not just about the money. If it were, you'd flip the coin and take your chances. Instead, we make constant tradeoffs that aim both to maximize our happiness and to minimize future handwringing over our decisions. Losses—even if merely imagined—weigh heavily on our psyches and profoundly inform our choices.

Happily, technology is a highly useful tool for managing this never-ending tightrope of difficult financial decisions, both big and small. If you are buying a house, you can check numerous real estate websites to evaluate your options. Considering the purchase of a new car or television? An Internet search will help you find the best price and let you read in-depth product reviews. Perhaps you are out on the town with friends. With your smartphone, you can check into every eatery nearby, find a highly rated one, and even book a table. In each case, technology allows you to maximize your choices and—just as importantly—minimize potential regret.

For all the clear benefits of technology in your daily life, chances are very good that you don't leverage it effectively, when it comes to investing. But why not? Part of the answer is obviously that nagging fear of regret. We worry that we'll make the wrong decision and lose part of our hard-earned capital with an ill-considered investment from a dubious source. A larger issue, however, is that the Internet is a "firehose" of information, and it is hard to know where to begin, and whom to trust.

When faced with an overwhelming array of choices, we tend to revert to the familiar ones even if they aren't the best options out there. In other words, despite a dizzying array of twenty-first century tech-enabled information resources, we tend to act on a limited menu of choices. To effectively balance the wealth of information available to us with our natural avoidance of regret, we need a clear and consistent strategy. Without such a playbook, our psychological tendency toward regret would be a permanent and unwelcomed third wheel.

Consider the topic of this book: social media and the investment process. Chances are that you know something about both, but they are difficult and complex topics. Keeping up with all the latest Internet outlets for individual social expression is a full-time job, and there seem to be new offerings every week. And investing is never easy, with the last decade's volatility only adding to the confusion.

A marriage of these two subjects of social media and investing might seem like an unholy alliance. But technology marches forward, and we must follow in its path. The good news is that you already have the skills and, if you've read this far, you clearly have the interest to succeed in this new challenge. There's even better news: You have an excellent guide on your journey with the author of this book, Brian Egger. I have known Brian for twenty years as a colleague and friend, and his ability to think clearly about the complex world of investing is first-rate. You are in good hands here.

The investment process in light of social media is an important topic for individual investors to understand. Even if you only choose to use a fraction of the contents of this book for your investment decisions, you will be better off for it. Institutional investors—"big money" hedge funds, mutual fund managers, pension funds, and very wealthy individuals—constantly scramble to leverage every possible advantage and reach their goals. Using social media is the single hottest topic for many of them at the moment. How—not if—they choose to incorporate this technology into their investment processes will play an increasingly important role in how they value securities in coming years. As an investor you need to understand these changes too, and that is the purpose of this book.

In the end, investing is simply a microcosm of our life's journey. We constantly make choices between two scarce resources: time and money. We proactively seek happiness while seeking to minimize regret. At the same time, the rules are always changing, and we have to change with them. Using every resource at our disposal, guided by those whom we trust, is the best way to navigate the investment landscape. The use of social media in investing is now part of the capital markets, so it must be on your roadmap.

After all, wouldn't you like to be that capricious rich uncle one day?

Nicholas Colas
Chief Market Strategist
ConvergEx Group

Introduction

Social Media: A Key to Stock Market Survival

In recent years, social media has become a linchpin for investment success. Mounting evidence suggests that the messages on Twitter and investing websites, such as StockTwits, can predict future stock market behavior. However, the importance of social media as an investing tool extends well beyond its predictive capacity. Twitter and other online communities are often the best source of insight into the causes of breakout moves in stocks. For a growing number of companies and research organizations, social media websites have become the venues of choice for communicating with investors about business trends. These websites are often the first and best sources for learning about the outcome of policy decisions that determine the fate of corporations. By using social media, investors may be able to learn about breaking news before it hits the mainstream media.

For those who might question whether or not *social media* can make them smarter investors, consider the alternative proposition that *media* can make them smarter investors. Very few investors I know would question the validity of that assertion. The problem seems to be with the "social" aspects of social media. As an investor, you must get past the perception that Twitter, Facebook, and YouTube are little more than virtual sandboxes for overgrown adolescents who are prone to idle gossip.

If you think social media has some growing up to do, and isn't quite ready for Wall Street, think again. An expanding segment of the investing population is embracing the value of the social web as a vehicle for learning more about investments and the stock market. Instances of corporate tweeting are becoming the rule rather than the exception. On January 16, 2014, retailer J.C. Penney rankled industry analysts when it announced that it would "begin breaking information" such as marketing campaigns or low-level employee hires exclusively through its Twitter account. J.C. Penney wants to have the flexibility to use Twitter to communicate with "the Street" without the "formality and time-consuming requirements of a press release."

The best way for investors to enter the fray of the rapidly evolving world of social finance is to become acquainted with some of the essential resources that are available online. This book is structured with that objective in mind. Chapter 1 provides some important context about the regulatory and business forces that have fueled the evolution of social media as an investing tool.

Chapter 2 features an introduction to the critical role that Twitter plays in investing, and details several elements of its website that can be streamlined for investment research. Chapter 3 introduces readers to the dynamic world of investing blogs and presents several examples of online journalism and financial writing, each having a different style.

Chapter 4 describes RSS feeds, which are online article syndication tools, and related applications (also referred to as apps) that facilitate the process of digesting streams of information from multiple blogs and social media sources. Chapter 5 presents several important examples of crowdsourced websites that can be used to obtain investment commentary, financial estimates, and stock recommendations from user communities.

Chapter 6 contains an introduction to some of the critical resources that are available on major financial websites, such as Yahoo! Finance. Chapter 7 features the dynamic world of financial webcasts, podcasts, and related audio-visual media that can enhance your understanding of the stock market.

In Chapter 8, I address the esoteric world of social bookmarking websites, such as reddit and Pinterest, which can be useful adjunct resources for investors. Chapter 9 explains the connection between "high-frequency trading" and the burgeoning world of social media analytics. Technology companies have developed novel approaches to gleaning sentiment signals from the mountains of data generated by Twitter and other social media websites, and this chapter details the essentials from an investment perspective.

In the book's tenth and final chapter, readers are presented with detailed examples of how investors can incorporate many of the social media tools discussed throughout the book into their daily investment research and trading. Finally, this book concludes with some predictions about what lies ahead for social media as an influence on the world of investing and a resource guide that notes the social media and financial websites and applications of today.

CHAPTER ONE

Why Social Media Is So Important for Investors

Some investors have already discovered the importance of social media as an investing resource. However, the world of social finance is still in its infancy. Recently, stock market observers have borne witness to several jarring examples of how messages on social media websites such as Twitter (*www.twitter.com*) can move markets. Yet many active users of social media resources are unaware of, or are underusing, the features that define these applications as financial and investment research tools. In other instances, individuals with a vested interest in the stock market are simply not tuned in to social media at all. This chapter highlights the contrast between the powerful influence of social media on financial markets and the limited extent to which it is currently being used by investors.

A Metaphor for Social Finance

Our galaxy, the Milky Way, and our closest galactic neighbor, Andromeda, will collide someday. That event has been predicted with near certainty by NASA, thanks to the Hubble Space

Telescope. According to NASA, Andromeda is approaching us at a velocity that is 2,000 times faster than a Major League pitcher's fastball. Even at that astounding speed, it will take about four billion years for the galactic collision to take place.

The worlds of investing and the Internet are also on a collision course, but investors won't have to wait billions of years to see its effects. It is already happening. These two big spheres of activity—investing and the Internet—both operate at a breakneck pace. They are beginning to coalesce, and we are awash in the disruptive ripple effects of their convergence. You don't need the Hubble Telescope to see this. Its effects can be detected with the naked eye.

On April 23, 2013, the Dow Jones Industrial Average dropped 145 points—a 1 percentage point move—then quickly recovered its entire loss, all in the space of about two minutes. This rare instance of market whiplash occurred in the cramped interval between 1:07 P.M. and 1:10 P.M. Those few panic-ridden minutes of trading were precipitated by a false rumor that President Obama had been injured by two explosions at the White House. The means by which the rumor spread was Twitter. It was quickly revealed that someone had hacked the Twitter account of the Associated Press and transmitted the phony news.

Instances of compromised e-mail and social media accounts are not uncommon. However, this bit of disturbing news raised the specter of a grave national security threat. It not only jarred onlookers but also erased and, just as quickly, restored, $136 billion in stock market value. Any trader working on Wall Street that day who had stepped away from his desk at 1:06 P.M. to go to the bathroom probably missed the entire rollercoaster ride.

This brief, scary instance of trading chaos would not have occurred without two contributing elements. First, the new unstructured, chaotic, irrepressible, and sometimes irresponsible world of social media has clashed with the U.S. securities market, a bastion of the "old economy." For those who had never used Twitter, the hackers' deception probably seemed like a sinister, high-tech prank by a comic book villain. But to the stock market, this hyperkinetic reaction to this tidbit of fake news was no joke. Computerized trading programs catalyzed events, even as human onlookers greeted the hacker-conceived rumor with a mix of skepticism and dread, and algorithmic systems hastened a selloff that left even market veterans in a brief state of shock.

Individual investors are but one group that must reckon with the maelstrom of social media and its effects on the investment markets. In April 2013, the *New York Times* highlighted the concerned reactions of members of the institutional investment community to the White House explosion rumor. Seasoned Wall Street traders must scramble to sort through a deluge of social media messages, separate the relevant from the meaningless, and distinguish between the accurate and the apocryphal. Financial service and media firms hire technology companies to help them filter through social media messages and identify those that are truly relevant.

In the wake of the Associated Press hacking debacle, it is not hard to imagine similarly fast, and equally disturbing, scenarios playing out again. Investors can prepare themselves for such unforeseen events by removing the veil of mystery that seems to be wrapped around the world of social media.

Many Internet Users Underuse Social Media's Investment Tools

According to a study by Pew Research Center, 73 percent of all Internet users are active on social media websites. According to the same study, which was published in 2012, an estimated 18 percent of all Internet users are active on Twitter. The fact that

Twitter has penetrated only a small percentage of the overall Internet-using population is evidence of its growth potential as a business and financial research tool. Internet user statistics reveal another important unrealized opportunity: Many investors who already use social media have not yet taken advantage of some of the basic, empowering attributes of Twitter.

An important feature of Twitter, one that is a particularly useful business tool, is the "hashtag"—the "#" symbol users sometimes place in front of a word or phrase to categorize it by its subject. Users can simply submit, and search for, messages that include a hashtag. Using hashtags helps ensure that one's tweets are easily found by other Twitter users during online searches. For example, investors searching on Twitter for information about investing might look under "#investing." Without the inclusion of hashtags, the searching process on Twitter is far less effective. Yet, according to a survey of mobile device users by RadiumOne, an online advertising firm, only 58 percent of consumers use hashtags on a regular basis. Even frequent users of social media often don't employ hashtags. Recently I asked a student audience how many of them use hashtags. A surprisingly small number of students—well less than half of those in attendance—said that they did.

Another important Internet tagging and search convention for investment research is the use of the "cashtag," represented by a dollar sign, paired with a stock symbol (e.g., "$GE" for General Electric). The importance of using cashtags—a social media notation that was pioneered by StockTwits and later adopted by Twitter—is discussed at length in Chapter 5.

Although the cashtag has become ubiquitous on investing website StockTwits (*www.stocktwits.com*), it is only in its early stages of adoption on Twitter. In October 2013, Statista, an online statistics portal, published its findings regarding the most discussed companies on Twitter, as measured by the mention of cashtags in tweets originated in August 2013. Not surprisingly, Apple, the U.S. company with the largest stock market value, topped Statista's list of the ten "most cashtagged" stocks. However, the use of cashtags was limited to a small group of securities. During August 2013, cashtag mentions for just three stocks—Apple Inc., Tesla Motors Inc., and BlackBerry Limited—accounted for approximately 60 percent of the total number of Twitter cashtag mentions observed for those top ten stocks. Although Apple, Tesla, and Blackberry dominated the "cashtag conversation" on Twitter, their stocks accounted for, in aggregate, only 32 percent of the total market value of all those top ten stocks.

A Wake-Up Call

Many seasoned individual investors were deeply affected by the burst of the dot-com bubble in 2000 and the great financial crisis of 2008. They became skeptical about financial advice and distrustful of financial advisors, and they question the motives of people who work on Wall Street. But mostly, they are pragmatists who want their money to work for them, rather than have it lie under a mattress, and they understand that interest income from money market accounts can't keep pace with inflation (even when inflation is as tame as they can remember). It is harder than ever to understand how the stock market works. There is something new and unsettling about how it functions.

When many people outside the world of finance think of the people who work on Wall Street, they come up with what may be unfair characterizations. They generally imagine Wall Streeters to be young and technologically savvy, perhaps even the coddled beneficiaries of the Information Age.

How much of social media you let into your life is, of course, your own choice. However, I hope that after finishing this book you will come away with an appreciation for how this technology can open doors for you as an investor.

There is a dizzying array of choices out there for those who want to tap the power of the Internet. You may be new to many of them. Just beneath the surface layer of social media—the Facebooks and Twitters—lies a substratum of quirky, lesser-known applications. They are instantly recognizable to some by their whimsical, colorful icons. They have names that are equally whimsical: reddit, Digg, Delicious, and StumbleUpon. They are often referred to as social bookmarking websites. As an investor, you may not use them, but you need to know that they exist.

In order to benefit from the information that is out there, there are a few things you need to understand about social media, particularly if you're new to it or have only used it a small amount.

First, you should know that social media is transforming the way information is conveyed to investors. We have all observed the informal way in which people communicate when they use e-mail and social media websites. The writing is punchy and laced with cryptic acronyms. Twitter cuts off all user messages at 140 characters, and so tweeted messages have an abbreviated, staccato-like rhythm. This new brand of shorthand has crept into business writing. The benefits and drawbacks of its succinctness are already affecting how companies address their stakeholders.

Second, you should know that powerful changes in the structure and operation of the stock market are unfolding. Just as the lightning-fast pace of Twitter message feeds can seem daunting to the individual investor, the dramatically accelerated speed at which stock trading takes place intimidates even seasoned stock market professionals. Today, computerized automation manages many aspects of what has long been a human institution.

According to the research and consulting firm, TABB Group, more than half of the U.S. equity trading volume can now be attributed to activity by hedge funds, high-frequency traders, and computerized algorithms. Many individual investors increasingly feel that stock market investing is something that's no longer "by them," or "for them." To them, the stock market has taken on a cold, mechanized feeling. As the *Wall Street Journal* aptly said, "Stocks aren't fun anymore; they are scary."

Many investment clubs—organizations that cater to the needs and interests of nonprofessional investors who have a passion for the stock market—are also at risk of falling behind in the new world of social finance. Last August, I walked over to my town library to attend a meeting of the local chapter of a statewide investment club. I entered the library's main meeting room, where I found eleven people sitting around a U-shaped table, shuffling through dog-eared printouts of dated *Value Line Investment Survey* stock reports. *Value Line* stock reviews have their place, and investment clubs are still important, but the world of investing has changed dramatically in the last twenty years. The need to find new, relevant information, and the ability to find it quickly, has made the use of the Internet imperative. Becoming better acquainted with some of the latest elements of consumer technology has never been more important.

Folks over Forty Have Much to Lose . . . and Gain

In April 2013, securities regulators permitted corporations to publish new financial data and news announcements on Twitter (*www.twitter.com*) and Facebook (*www.facebook.com*). This event makes it more important than ever for you to develop some facility with using social media websites. Ultimately, it doesn't matter if you're old or young—to be successful in the market, you must interact with it the way it is now. It is critical that you understand the current investor demographics, and how each group engages the market.

At the moment, the majority of stocks and bonds in the United States is held by older investors. About 75 percent of stocks and bonds in the United States are owned by households headed by someone over the age of forty. What about mutual funds? Researchers Michael Bogdan and Daniel Schrass found that about 40 percent of those assets belong to households in which someone fifty-five or older makes the financial decisions for the family.

Percentage of US Households Owning Equities or Bonds by Head of Household Age, 2008

Exhibit 1: Equity and Bond Owner Characteristics by Age
Source: Investment Company Institute (ICI) and Securities Industry and Financial Markets Association (SIFMA), 2008.

Many Wall Street professionals are younger adults, in their twenties and thirties. The securities industry is, in many respects, a younger person's profession. The business of owning stocks and bonds? Not so much. Households headed by the members of Generation X and Generation Y—those born since 1965—own only about one-third of all equities and bonds. In other words, the age group principally associated with the profession of buying and selling stocks does not own a lot of stocks, relative to other population segments.

Let's look at the north and south generational poles of the population: those over sixty-five, and those under forty. The average household headed by a senior citizen has $350,000 in stock and bond holdings. That's about *six times* the dollar amount of those particular financial assets held by families whose financial decisions are made by someone under age forty.

US Household Ownership of Equities or Bonds by Head of Household Age, 2008

	Younger than 40	65 and Older
Median household financial assets inside and outside employee-sponsored retirement plans	$60,000	$350,000
Median household financial assets in traditional or Roth IRAs	$12,500	$100,000

Exhibit 2: Household Financial Assets by Age
Source: Investment Company Institute (ICI) and Securities Industry and Financial Markets Association (SIFMA), 2008.

So much for stock ownership, which is clearly dominated by those with gray hair on their temples. How about Internet use? Perhaps it should be no surprise that this is where older Americans lag behind their younger counterparts. In fact, these older Americans use the Internet to access financial information only about *half* as often as people under forty years old. An estimated 82 percent of those under age forty go online to engage in financial transactions or find financial information (see Exhibit 3). Less than half of the sixty-five-and-older crowd does this.

Percentage of US Households Owning Equities or Bonds by Head of Household Age, 2008

	Younger than 40	65 and Older
Any type of financial-related use online	82%	47%
Accessed financial accounts	69%	34%
Accessed financial news online	64%	31%

Exhibit 3: Finance-Related Internet Use by Age
Source: Investment Company Institute (ICI) and Securities Industry and Financial Markets Association (SIFMA), 2008.

In the case of social media adoption, striking differences persist in user rates among younger and older Americans. Although 86 percent of all Internet users in the eighteen- to twenty-nine-year-old age group use Facebook, the same can be said of only 35 percent of Internet users older than age sixty-five. Note that this 35 percent adoption rate applies to senior citizens who *already use* the Internet. The percentage of all seniors who use Facebook probably hovers around 20 percent.

When it comes to Twitter, there's an even bigger disparity between old and young users. Pew Research estimates that 27 percent of the eighteen- to twenty-nine-year-old online population uses Twitter, in comparison to only 2 percent of Internet users in the sixty-five-plus age category.

Because they're less familiar with social media, middle-aged and older individuals bear the greatest risk of being left behind as more companies begin to announce corporate developments on Twitter and Facebook. However, younger individuals, even if they already use Twitter, are less likely to make informed financial decisions if they are unaware of the social media tools now being employed by investment professionals.

Most Twitter users who engage the social media website primarily as a personal communications tool are unfamiliar with how money managers use social media analytics. Even active Twitter users might not realize that potentially market-moving discussions now occur routinely on social bookmarking websites, such as reddit (*www.reddit.com*), or by way of video and audio recordings found on YouTube (*www.youtube.com*) and iTunes. A December 2013 article in the *Wall Street Journal* describes the growing prominence of technology firms such as Social Market Analytics (*www.social marketanalytics.com*). This type of technology firm "scans tweets for words that indicate sentiment around a stock," and scores "how the chatter around a particular stock is changing."

By now you are probably tripping over all the statistics cited in this chapter. But the specific numbers aren't as important as the key takeaway: Once companies start using social media to speak to the investing public, it is probable that many individual investors won't be listening and will be left behind in the process. That makes it doubly important that you learn as much as possible about how to use social media to improve your investing decisions.

Key Takeaways from Chapter One

- Due to changes in regulation and technology, social media applications, such as Twitter, are transforming the way information is conveyed to investors.
- More than half of U.S. equity trading volume can now be attributed to activity by social media–savvy hedge funds and high-frequency traders who use algorithms.
- Many Internet users who visit Twitter fail to take advantage of that website's powerful business and investment research tools, such as hashtags and cashtags.
- Households headed by someone age forty or older own about 75 percent of U.S. stocks or bonds, and *less than 10 percent* of Internet users over fifty are on Twitter.

CHAPTER TWO

How Twitter Is Transforming the World of Investing

Among leading social media websites, Twitter (*www.twitter.com*) has emerged as a particularly influential online resource for investors. Recent academic studies affirm Twitter's potential to predict stock market sentiment and stock price moves. However, its role in social finance did not emerge in a vacuum. Several important business and regulatory developments hastened the emergence of Twitter as an important financial communications medium. In this chapter I explain that business and regulatory context. I then provide three important examples of how stock market professionals use Twitter to illustrate how all investors can get the most out of Twitter. I conclude by examining why some people are reluctant to use Twitter—and note a simple suggestion that can help individual investors overcome that resistance.

Rinse and Retweet: The Day Apple Soared

On August 13, 2013, the share price of Apple (*www.apple.com*) jumped 5 percent on about two and a half times its average daily trading volume. Of course, a big trading move by the world's most valuable publicly traded company drew the attention of the investing world. The involvement of a fabled activist investor, whose announcement of a large stake in the consumer electronics giant helped lift its stock above $70 (adjusted for a 7-to-1 stock split that occurred in June 2014) for the first time in months, further dramatized the event.

Viewers of cable news would not have been surprised to learn that some swashbuckling young rogue of the hedge-fund world was responsible for buoying Apple's then-floundering stock price. However, the real story behind the breakout move in Apple shares proved to be a jolting revelation for Wall Street watchers on that hazy late-summer day.

Two key elements of the Apple stake announcement are worthy of reflection. First, the venue that had been selected to disseminate the news announcement was Twitter. Second, the scrappy, social media–savvy trader whose stake in Apple had roiled trading activity on an otherwise quiet August afternoon was only two and a half years shy of celebrating his eightieth birthday. His name is Carl Icahn.

Mr. Icahn's announcement, while jarring to the stock market, was not quite a bolt from the blue. The day before his now-famous tweet, Icahn had issued a press release announcing his intention "to use Twitter from time to time to communicate with the public about our company and other issues."

Icahn Enterprises, by acknowledging that some of its future tweets could be considered material information, was giving a nod to a recent pronouncement by the Securities and Exchange Commission (SEC). That SEC ruling had given Icahn a green light to use his Twitter handle to disseminate corporate announcements. In the wake of the SEC's actions, other companies have turned to Twitter as a means of communicating with investors and the news media. For example, in April 2013, Zillow, Inc., a real estate services company, became the first corporation to take earnings conference call questions on Twitter and Facebook. During the same month, Zynga Inc., a social games company, announced that it may begin to communicate material information on Twitter and Facebook.

Regulators Muddy the Waters

The SEC's anointment of Twitter as an acceptable medium for financial communications might have seemed improbable even a year before Carl Icahn used the application to announce his ownership of Apple stock. Why did regulators decide to validate Twitter—a pioneer of social media—as a way for companies to send new information to investors? The answer requires some context.

In August 2000, the SEC issued Regulation FD (Fair Disclosure). The rule required publicly traded companies to announce material information to all investors, and to the public, at the same time, and to do so by using "acceptable methods." Prior to the ruling only certain well-connected analysts and investors had been privy to an early peek at company data. The SEC issued the ruling to level the playing field for individual investors and make markets more egalitarian.

At the turn of the millennium, there had been agreement among regulators about which media were appropriate for disseminating financial news. Companies were already expected to announce material events by filing a special form, known as an 8-K, with the SEC. Other outlets were also considered acceptable for disclosing new information. Those included press releases through major news services and conference calls or press conferences (as long as those events were open to the public).

By 2000, the SEC had become aware that many companies were using their corporate websites to post press releases. The SEC was not ready to permit companies to broadcast information to the public exclusively on their Internet websites. This meant that executives still had to distribute copies of the release to media outlets as well so that non–Internet users wouldn't be blindsided by market-moving news. However, the Commission realized that using the Internet to post announcements would likely gain more acceptance once more U.S. households went online.

Fast forward thirteen years: The same SEC that had been skittish about allowing companies to rely exclusively on the Internet for broadcasting news was now ready to open the floodgates. By allowing corporations to communicate on Twitter, the Commission seemed prepared to skirt the edge of the Internet's new frontier. What had prompted the Commission to validate Twitter as a medium for talking to investors? The actions of one corporate executive with an itchy "Twitter finger" had forced the SEC to show its hand.

In July 2012, Netflix's CEO, Reed Hastings, decided to use his personal Twitter account to boast that his company's monthly online views had exceeded one billion hours. Netflix had not reported this business anecdote in a press release. Neither the company, nor its CEO, had ever previously used Twitter or Facebook to communicate with its investors, or announce business results.

The unusual move by Netflix's CEO stirred a lot of controversy. Most observers criticized Hastings for using his personal account to reveal news about a public company. However, Hastings's use of Twitter was seen by some as a forward-thinking acknowledgment that nontraditional media had gained legitimacy in the corporate world. Detractors of Netflix's actions were quick to point out that large segments of the investing public had never used Twitter.

In April 2013, after reviewing the actions of Netflix's CEO, the SEC affirmed that companies could use Facebook or Twitter to announce new information. The SEC's only prerequisite was that investors had to be notified in advance about which social media platform would be used to disclose data.

From time to time, the SEC has been the target of criticism about its failure to keep pace with new technologies such as the Internet. The irony of the Commission's reaction to Reed Hastings's online boast was that, by trying to protect individual investors, it may have made things worse. Because the use of Twitter so clearly skewed in the direction of younger people, the SEC's actions might actually have reinforced the clubby exclusivity of Wall Street. And, indeed for many on Main Street, this action only confirmed suspicions that the securities industry is a fraternity of twenty- and thirty-something-year-old MBAs with an unfair edge over the general public.

Three Ways *All* Investors Can Use Twitter

Even newcomers to Twitter can follow some simple guidelines that should enable them to glean valuable information and insights from the social media platform. You would be well served by following financial professionals and journalists who share valuable insights on Twitter. You can also obtain useful information by conducting searches on Twitter that incorporate the hashtag and cashtag conventions introduced in Chapter 1. You may also want to peruse Twitter lists to identify topical tweets about investing, as well as new tweeters who might be worth following.

Technique One: Follow the Leaders

Twitter blends the running narrative of a blog with the one-on-one connectivity and real-time updates of an e-mail system. Opening a Twitter account is free and easy to do. It takes only minutes to join the conversation.

Twitter is equipped with a search capability that allows you to look up past tweets associated with other Twitter accounts. While Twitter, like e-mail, was conceived as a two-way communication tool, there's nothing—absolutely nothing—to stop you from following (that is, receiving tweets from) other users on Twitter and *never* sending a single tweet yourself.

The perception of Twitter as a microcosm of gossipy chatter and racy uploaded photographs—a view that is not entirely undeserved—stems from its social roots. However, the underlying reality is that it is a rapidly evolving entity. An increasing number of corporate executives and high-profile financiers have taken to Twitter to share their views, both business and personal.

What has emerged is a blend of insipid personal banter, off-color jokes, quirky film clips, as well as occasional nuggets of surprisingly thoughtful commentary. Much of the most interesting material comes from important opinion leaders. To sort through the frivolous chatter, you can simply choose to follow individuals whose perspective and insights seem most valuable to you.

Whom you choose to follow on Twitter is entirely up to you. To inform your understanding of investing, you might choose to follow the Twitter posts of leading business journalists or investors. Or you might prefer instead to track prominent economists or market strategists.

It would have taken an act of unusual prescience—and perhaps some clairvoyance—to have joined the ranks of Carl Icahn's 65,400 Twitter followers back in August 2013, and received his now-famous tweet about investing in Apple (see Exhibit 4). Fortunately, you didn't have to be one of those to whom he tweeted directly: Right after the investor fessed up about his slice of Apple, Twitter was ablaze with a series of retweets. Followers of Icahn copied and rebroadcasted his message to their own followers, many of whom, in turn, did the same thing.

Exhibit 4: Carl Icahn's Twitter Profile in August 2013
Source: *www.Twitter.com.*

Social media neophytes will quickly discover the variability in the frequency and style of tweeting by Twitter users. While Carl Icahn's words can move markets, as of this writing he had only 132 tweets to his name. Other individuals spew forth tweets with an almost obsessive regularity.

The result of this wide-ranging set of user habits is that your Twitter homepage is likely to feature a disproportionately large number of messages from more prolific users. Those frequent posts might seem to drown out the tweets from others who use this medium more selectively. The good news is that you can easily modify your Twitter preferences by following new accounts and deleting others. You might base your preferences on the quality of content, and other times you might base it on the frequency or intermittence of messages.

Some high-profile Twitter users, including corporate leaders, are all business when they use social networking applications. Other business luminaries aren't the least bit shy about mixing serious-minded comments with jokes, anecdotes, political banter, or the occasional "regular guy" rant (e.g., "waiting in line at the DMV is like watching paint dry—LOL").

Twitter's 140-character message limit transforms even the most thoughtful users into stream-of-consciousness stenographers. A few writers will inevitably end up sounding like they are incoherent babblers when they communicate in this fashion. Other Twitter users can convey important ideas and facts with an unadorned clarity and terseness that can't be found elsewhere. In either event, the confessional nature of Twitter is revealing in a way that traditional media is not.

Technique Two: "Cashtag, You're It!"

Even if you're not currently a Twitter user, you've probably searched the Internet for something already: a restaurant, a movie, the birth date of a celebrity, or maybe the directions to a vacation spot. For at least some of these searches, you probably used the biggest search engine of them all, Google (*www.google.com*). Like Google, Twitter is equipped with a powerful search algorithm. To conduct a Twitter search, simply type a search term in the box on the top of a Twitter screen that is marked with a small magnifying glass (the universal icon for Internet-based searching).

There are several symbols you can use to target and optimize searches on Twitter. Perhaps you're looking for another user of Twitter whom you want to follow. If so, the Twitter address you type should be preceded by the "@" symbol. Assuming you type the correct address for that Twitter account, the owner's profile will be rendered on your screen. You can choose to receive tweets from that individual or company by clicking the Follow button with the little blue bird next to it. Once you begin to follow that tweeter, your homepage (accessible by clicking the house icon on the upper-left corner of the screen) will include that account holder's tweets in your Twitter feed (i.e., the timeline of all tweets from individuals whom you have chosen to follow).

If you've never used Twitter before, let's demystify another symbol: the oft-mentioned and insidery-sounding "hashtag." (I mentioned this in Chapter 1.)

A hashtag is a Twitter search word or topic denoted by the "#" symbol. Twitter users place a hashtag symbol in front of a word or phrase to categorize it by its subject. Other Twitter users can search for tweets on this same topic, either by typing "#[search term]" in their search box, or by clicking a hashtagged word in the body of someone else's tweet, where it is highlighted so that readers can easily tell that it is an interactive link.

TWEETING YOUR VOTE

If you watch reality television shows, you have no doubt observed contestants competing for the votes of fans. The announcer might invite responses on Twitter, accompanied by something like "hashtag vote." In order to respond to that poll, you enter the term "#vote" anywhere in your message, and that sent tweet then joins others categorized under the same hashtag symbol.

Hashtags can be powerful search tools for business as well. For example, as an investor if you want to do some research on Apple's stock and learn more about one of its key products, the iPhone, you can search Twitter under the term "#iPhone." The search will render a reverse chronologically ordered list (i.e., newest entry first) of all tweets with "#iPhone" in the body of the text.

Twitter breaks down its search results into three categories: "Top," "All," and "People you follow." The Top results are those that are popular with other users—who have interacted with them either by replying to them, retweeting their messages, or denoting them as a favorite. If you prefer *not* to have search results narrowed down in this way, select the All option. Alternatively, you may prefer to limit your search for hashtagged tweets to only those individuals whom you have chosen to follow.

"Cashtag" is a newer feature of Twitter, one particularly relevant to investors. We also talked about this in Chapter 1. Like hashtags, cashtags can be used to organize and narrow down Twitter-based searches. As the name suggests, cashtags are created by placing the "$" symbol before a relevant search term. A cashtag-denoted search term must always be a stock symbol.

Cashtags as a financial-search shorthand were first used by the investing website StockTwits. This site was cofounded by Howard Lindzon, a hedge-fund manager and early-stage company investor. Lindzon is one of a pioneering group of institutional investors who, for some time, has tapped the power of Twitter for stock research purposes. In July 2012, Twitter, aware of the growing use of the dollar sign–denoted search convention, began to organize searchable tweets denoted by cashtags.

StockTwits is part of a family of investment-related websites that rose to prominence by curating financial message streams from its members, as well as from other social media sources. As with many social media applications, you can integrate StockTwits with your Facebook, LinkedIn, or Google accounts. We'll talk more about StockTwits and other online curators as social media intermediaries in Chapter 5.

On July 30, 2012, Twitter announced its decision to enable cashtag-based searches. The company did so with little fanfare by tweeting the news (see Exhibit 5). The irony of Twitter playing catch-up with a search convention that the company itself had spawned illustrates just how influential Twitter has become, not only in the world of popular culture, but also in the world of business.

Exhibit 5: Twitter, Inc.'s Cashtag Announcement
Source: *www.Twitter.com.*

The retweets that followed Twitter's prosaic cashtag announcement included those of many users who shrugged off the news, because they had already been conducting Twitter searches with cashtags. The lesson here is that you should not feel the least bit self-conscious about being a late adopter of Twitter or other social media applications. After all, Twitter's cashtag announcement is a notable case of a social media pioneer that ended up playing catch-up with itself!

As an individual investor, even if you are equipped with some of the powerful search tools discussed in this chapter, trying to tap the wealth of data stored on Twitter will likely yield a lot of search results—perhaps more than you are able to digest. You can learn to be selective when you review old tweets in order to find valuable new information.

Like other search-rendered content on the Internet, there's plenty of junky stuff out there: off-topic remarks, jokes, unfounded opinions, half-baked insights, and rumors, some of which were crafted to serve the interests of their originators. Over time, you can develop the judgment that will enable you to frame search terms in order to yield more useful results. Filtering through searches to find useful content is a skill you need to develop to become an effective stock researcher, whether you choose to do this on your own or with the aid of online curating tools, such as those discussed in Chapter 5.

Technique Three: Learn More with Lists

A list is defined by Twitter's website as "a curated group of Twitter users." The advantage of following a list on Twitter is that you can obtain access to a customized Twitter timeline, with messages *only* from those tweeters who share your interest in a specific field. If you elect to "subscribe" to a list, then that list will begin to appear on your personal profile page. By clicking that list name at any future date, you can obtain access to the most recent tweets generated by the like-minded members of the list, as well as the Twitter profile summaries of those members.

How do you decide which lists to join? One approach is to visit the Twitter profile pages of individuals whom you already follow and whose insights and expertise seem particularly valuable to you. On the bottom of each Twitter account holder's profile page, below their most recent tweets and photographs, you can find a series of clickable menu categories, including that individual's Twitter followers; the names of the Twitter members whom they follow; as well as the lists to which they have subscribed. While a large percentage of Twitter account holders are not members of, or subscribers to, any lists, the lists with which tweeters affiliate themselves can say a lot about their professional and personal passions.

Investors with an interest in social finance might be interested in subscribing to Twitter lists that focus on social media, financial websites, and investment conferences. You should periodically review the tweets filed under each of these lists to make sure that you haven't missed something important. You can also peruse the Twitter member profiles affiliated with these lists to find new individuals whom you may want to follow.

How Stock Market Professionals Use Twitter

To see what using Twitter looks like in practice, let's examine three examples of investors in action on Twitter.

Going Rogue

The freewheeling culture of Twitter has been filtering into the compliance-focused world of Wall Street, where analysts at large brokerage firms are subject to numerous regulatory constraints that affect how research is conducted and communicated. Several independent stock analysts—those not affiliated with investment banks and broker-dealers—have tapped into new audiences by using Twitter and other social media.

One prominent independent analyst and prolific Twitter user, Brian Sozzi of Belus Capital Advisors, has made a name for himself through an aggressive campaign of retail store "channel checks." Channel checks refer to an analyst's technique for gaining insights into the business conditions of a subject company by interviewing, observing, and analyzing data from its suppliers, customers, and competitors. Twitter's ability to blend short written commentary with photographs and videos lends itself well to this research process.

Sozzi's candid, and sometimes controversial, observations about store layouts and appearances have gained the attention of Twitter watchers. Financial media outlet Benzinga (*www.benz inga.com*) included Sozzi on its list of the best finance people to follow on Twitter. Sozzi's Belus Capital Advisors markets a series of subscription-based research products, including the *Rumor Mill*, for which it charges $15 per month, and a broader set of offerings that cost approximately $800 per year. However, individuals can obtain free access to Sozzi's Twitter messages and to his website blog, *The Water Cooler*.

Sozzi's *Water Cooler* blog posts are filled with the photographs and videos that have become a staple of his brand of channel checking. His photographs of stores operated by Walmart, J.C. Penney, Target, McDonald's, and Sears have stirred controversy because they include unflattering images of barren shelves, outdated signs, uninviting restaurant seating, leaky car batteries, and stockrooms in disarray.

In one incident, which *Business Week* chronicled in a story that labeled Sozzi a "guerrilla stock analyst," the Belus Capital Advisors researcher rankled financial executives at Sears. His photographs of empty store shelves and unattractive product displays also appeared in a separate article on the website *TheStreet* (*www.thestreet.com*). The published images elicited a defensive response from the head of corporate communications at Sears, who tweeted that he was "trying to infuse some balance into [*TheStreet's*] reporting." He also chided Sozzi for using "cheap shots to increase his @klout score." (Klout [*www.klout.com*] scores are widely followed measures of social media influence.)

The Sears executive went on to write that "we can't let the shorts and others with an agenda simply take uncontested shots at us." In the ensuing exchange of messages on Twitter, prompted by Sears's response to Sozzi and *TheStreet*, some individuals cheered Sears's defense of the quality of its stores and corporate management, while other observers praised Sozzi for his rigorous store checks and analytic candor.

The *Business Week* account of Sozzi's standoff with Sears quotes the analyst as saying that he is "redefining what an analyst can and should be in the crowdsourced age of social media, where everyone with a smartphone can be a valuable, motivated contributor to real-time company analysis." Sozzi observed further that "there are real-time discussions happening on Twitter, Instagram, Facebook, and Vine on public companies . . . that deserve to be sourced to see if there are positive or negative surprises in the future financial results." Sozzi's pointed investment conclusion—that "Sears is seeking to slowly liquidate itself by closing stores"—resonated, in part, because it was punctuated by memorable visual images.

Whatever your take on the conduct of the principals in this exchange, most observers would agree that it underscores the power of Twitter as a medium for sharing information, images, and opinions. If you had exposure to Sears's stock, you might be well served by following both Sozzi and Sears's corporate communications department on Twitter. The issues raised by independent analysts and journalists on Twitter, and the responses from company executives, form part of the backdrop against the decisions that all investors must make about the stocks they own.

Waving the Flag for Twitter

Josh Brown is a financial advisor, a frequent guest speaker on CNBC, and the flamboyant author of the popular investment blog *The Reformed Broker* (*www.thereformedbroker.com*). His important role as an investment blogger is discussed in Chapter 3. With nearly 78,000 followers on Twitter, and a similar number of tweets to his name, Brown has emerged as a leading voice in the social finance community and an advocate of using Twitter to become a better investor. In December 2013, Brown published a blog entry titled, "Can You Get Investment Knowledge from Twitter?" This blog post might strike some readers as blunt and prosaic. However, it lays out Brown's assessment of the value of Twitter, and does so with the bare-knuckles candor for which he has become well known.

Brown views Twitter as an effective tool that helps users keep up with investment trends and controversies, and understand how stock market participants are reacting to important news and data. He also uses the medium to become better informed about financial topics and to communicate with other traders, analysts, advisors, and corporate executives. What is equally notable is how Brown does *not* use Twitter. He eschews "following traders into stock ideas and paying attention to their exits, entries, track records, boasts and brags." He also dismisses the value of Twitter as a source of stock market tips, which "can be fun and entertaining or costly and dangerous, depending on whether they're used and how."

Election Day Epiphany

Although I had already been using Twitter for stock research, its importance as an investing tool became tangibly apparent to me on November 6, 2012. As a securities analyst specializing in gambling and leisure stocks, I spend a considerable amount of time monitoring regulatory and political events that affect casino operators. While awaiting the outcome of the 2012 U.S. presidential election, I was keeping a close eye on my Twitter feed. Twitter had become my portal for tracking the outcome of a state ballot initiative that could dramatically affect the Mid-Atlantic casino industry.

By that evening, voters in Maryland decided the fate of casino gambling in their state. Passage of the state's Gaming Expansion Referendum authorized a new casino in Maryland's Prince George's County, a widely sought-after regional license, because of its proximity to Washington, D.C., and that city's demographically attractive suburbs. The passing of the referendum also permitted the state's existing casinos to operate table games, such as blackjack and craps.

The outcome of the ballot measure was a key development for investors in Penn National Gaming. Penn's highest-grossing casino, accounting for about one-fourth of its profits, was the Hollywood Casino at Charles Town Races in West Virginia. Maryland's approval of gaming expansion paved the way for competitor MGM Resorts International to build a casino at Maryland's National Harbor. An MGM casino at the National Harbor site, just seventy-five miles from Charles Town Races, could materially cannibalize Penn's lucrative West Virginia property.

In preparation for that political contest, I had begun following the Twitter accounts of several reporters at the *Washington Post* and the *Baltimore Sun* who cover Maryland politics. Shortly after the polls closed on Election Day that evening, tweets began scrolling across the screen of my iPad. The gaming expansion ballot initiative passed by a fifty-two to forty-eight margin, an outcome only later reported online by several local newspapers.

By following the tweets of a handful of reporters with specialized knowledge of the Maryland ballot contest, I had the benefit of receiving real-time updates on its status. My sense of the referendum's outcome and implications could not have been better informed, even if I had been sitting in a reporter's office as he monitored precinct-by-precinct voter returns.

Getting Stock News on Twitter? Get Serious!

All this talk about phony AP news alerts, clever hashtags, and Reed Hastings's online boasts might leave some of you feeling that Twitter's impact on the stock market is just a quirky aspect of the unbridled energy of social media. However, Twitter's potential effects on the financial world, and its possible predictive powers, have been the topic of some serious discussion in the faculty clubs of major universities.

In 2011, three professors at Indiana University published a study in the *Journal of Computational Science* on the relationship between the general mood of tweets and the movements of the stock market. The authors of this academic study looked at nearly 10 million tweets and found that certain emotional states such as "calmness" and "happiness" can predict a positive move in the Dow Jones Industrial Average.

For the average investor, the possibility that the prevailing mood of Twitter messages can serve as a crystal ball for stock market investment might not have much practical use. However, we live in a world of big data. New investment firms have the ability to canvass the Internet for tidbits of information that might serve as sentiment indicators. Equipped with the right technology, data-driven firms have the ability to scan the web's metadata for potential indicators of upward or downward stock price moves.

Even so, the firms that engage in this business of data sifting are neither clairvoyant nor immune to challenges. The market's scary reaction to the false rumors about a possible White House terror incident, mentioned in Chapter 1, provides but one example. Indeed, Twitter and its social media brethren have become potential breeding grounds for rumors and manipulative hoaxes. Nonetheless, in an era of high-frequency trading and rapid-fire stock transactions, the ability of trading houses to distinguish between fact and fiction can mean the difference between enormous gains in wealth and astonishing losses. In either case, and for better or for worse, individual investors who ride the coattails of powerful hedge funds and high-speed traders are along for the trip.

Twitter's Generational and Cultural Divide

Some Internet users regard the popular preoccupation with Facebook and Twitter as a form of narcissism. Outside the use of these applications to market their businesses and websites, many corporate professionals feel that there is something undisciplined, even unseemly, about sharing the unvarnished minutiae of their personal life with an audience of often-distant online acquaintances.

Source: Tailwind, *www.tailwindapp.com*. Reprinted with the permission of Danny Maloney, CEO of Tailwind.

It is unfair to arbitrarily dismiss any group's limited appetite for social media, like Twitter, as being synonymous with their discomfort with technology. For many computer users, it is simply not natural to share personal details with candor and abandon. If you are a light user of technology and social media, I don't expect this book to convert you into an obsessive tweeter. However, you can widen your horizons by becoming a Twitter "spectator." You can also do this without feeling the need to shake off your discomfort with sharing too much online.

You can be a keen observer of what is said on the Internet and still choose to reveal little about your own views and thoughts. While this approach to using Twitter and other Internet-based applications might strike some veteran users as anti-social, social media community participants should not feel an unnatural sense of obligation to share personal or professional information.

Bear in mind the motives of those who choose to engage the world of social media. These motives are sometimes laced with self-interest. Carl Icahn, for his part, has nearly 169,000 Twitter followers, but only follows the tweets of 108 other individuals (many of whom are financial news personalities). While his recent Apple tweet reverberated across the equity markets, as previously mentioned, he has only originated 132 Twitter messages to date. His use of Twitter is self-serving. In the same spirit, there is no reason why you shouldn't consider using Twitter with unabashed self-interest.

Takeaways from Chapter Two

- In April 2013, the SEC altered the regulatory landscape by affirming that companies can use Facebook and Twitter to announce new financial information.
- In order to sort through the frivolous chatter on Twitter, you can choose to follow individuals whose perspectives and insights you deem most valuable.
- Like "#"-denoted hashtags, cashtags (e.g., "$TWTR") can be used to narrow down Twitter-based searches for information about particular companies that interest you.

- Professional investors use Twitter to communicate the findings of their research channel checks, track business trends, and gauge how other market participants react to news and data.
- Evidence suggests that Twitter messages, if properly vetted for accuracy, might be able to predict future stock market sentiment.

CHAPTER THREE

Getting Familiar with Financial Blogs

Business and financial blogs have become important sources of investment news, information, and insight. These blogs have several common structural features, explained in this chapter, that qualify them as a form of social media. In this chapter we'll consider several popular financial blogs that cover a wide range of investment topics, as well as specialized blogs that cater to investors who focus on specific subjects and industries. Finally, we'll discuss the importance of assessing the authenticity and possible motives of blog authors.

Why Are Business Blogs So Important?

The financial blogosphere (i.e., the collected community of financial blogs) is an eclectic world. Writers of investment blogs range from traditional business journalists to gossipy conspiracy theorists. Several years ago, the UK-based website Mindful Money (*www.mindfulmoney.com*) referred to the interlacing network of financial blogs on the web as "a carnivalesque conversation which mashes up genres such as news and reportage, blogs, satire, polemic, academic research, data visualization, and complex information processing."

When I talk about blogs, I'm not referring to personal websites devoted to the owner's love of cats or passion for vintage automobiles. Instead, I am referring to online publications that often provide useful insights and perspectives not found in traditional print and online publications. Mindful Money, for example, notes that "following new influentials on the social Web can offer 'the story behind the story' with more in-depth, consistent coverage, as well as covering stories before they break in the mainstream media." In other words, business blogs have their place on the reading list of any informed investor.

Recent investor survey findings suggest that financial blogs are likely to play an increasingly important role in the decisions made by stock market participants. In October 2013, The Brunswick Group, a business communications and corporate relations firm, conducted a survey of the use of social media by professional investors in the United States, Europe, and Asia. According to the survey, 25–28 percent of responding investors in those jurisdictions had made an investment decision based on content they first encountered in a blog post. Seventy percent of the survey's respondents indicated that they expect digital media to play a larger role in their future investment decisions.

How Do Financial Bloggers Make Money?

You might wonder, while skimming some of these blogs, whether the authors are paid to write them. The answer in most cases is no. While some bloggers charge a subscription fee for access to premium content on their websites, the underlying business model of most blogs remains rooted in online advertising. Blog writers invariably formalize a relationship with Google's AdSense division. Blog publishers place snippets of code supplied by Google on their web pages. This code activates advertisements from third parties who want to showcase their products or services to a given blogger's audience.

If a blog visitor is interested in the content of a particular advertisement, and decides to click through the text or image ad featured on the blogger's web page, then the blog publisher receives a portion of the revenues earned by Google for its role in facilitating the mouse click of that prospective online customer. These revenues are determined on a "pay per click" basis. Because only about 1 percent of most websites' visitors, on average, decide to click on one of these ads, it takes a large viewership to generate a revenue base sufficient to transform a blog into a profitable enterprise.

What Makes Blogs "Social"?

The inclusion of the subject of blogs in a book about social media resources for investors requires some explanation. There are several features that distinguish blogs from articles written by traditional print journalists. These features are what make these blogs "social."

The first distinguishing feature is that blog posts are appended with reader comments. For popular blogging sites, the word count of the Comments section of a particular article might exceed the length of the original blog post. The second characteristic of most blogs is the inclusion of a social sharing and voting mechanism. At the end of most blog posts, you'll find the familiar icons of leading social media websites. These icons, which are also referred to as widgets, enable users to share blog posts with, or recommend them to, others with a mouse click. These social sharing and voting widgets include LinkedIn's "Share" widget, Facebook's "Like" icon, Twitter's "Tweet" button, and Google's "+1" icon.

These social media selections enable you to express your favorable view of the blog post (with a Like or +1), or to share the blog post with your own social media networks. For example, if you encounter a blog post that you find informative and pertinent, you can click the Tweet icon, which activates a portal to your Twitter account. This generates a new tweet that includes a link to the blog post you selected. These sharing and voting functions are essential to the social nature of blogs. By choosing to share another blogger's article via Twitter, you can add the content of that blog article to your own running social media commentary.

The Value of Retweeting

Recalling the discussion about Twitter in the previous chapter, you might discover that many widely followed users of Twitter include, among their outgoing messages, a large number of retweets of other bloggers' comments. Effective users of Twitter rely on the application to originate their own ideas and comments, but they also use it to "curate" other observations from around the blogosphere that they find useful, insightful, or just amusing.

The social media icons at the end of blog articles are generally accompanied by callout windows that include numbers. These numerical designations indicate how many previous users elected to share, or vote in favor of, the article. If you're considering reading the original blog post, you can gauge the popularity and perhaps utility of that article based on the number of Likes, tweets, or Shares that the post has already garnered from other readers. Popular blog articles—including those that have already diffused into the larger blogosphere—usually carry large social media voting and sharing counts.

Breaking Down the Financial Blogosphere

Because there are so many financial blogs, you may find it useful to break down the unwieldy clumps of website offerings into subcategories. While it is difficult to make generalizations, the unruly world of online investment writing can be deconstructed into several archetypes. Here we'll look at four very different types of investment blogs, each of which has something unique to offer its readers. It is unlikely that all four of these online sources will appeal to you, but you might find one or more of them very informative. The four examples discussed in this chapter are *Zero Hedge*; *Seeking Alpha*; Felix Salmon, who was until recently affiliated with the international news agency Reuters (*www.reuters.com*); and the author of the *Reformed Broker* blog, Josh Brown, whom the *New York Times* once nicknamed the "Merchant of Snark."

Four Types of Investment Blogs

The bloggers who are profiled in this chapter cover a wide range of financial and economic topics, and offer readers a diversity of perspectives and writing approaches. Some blogs, such as *Zero Hedge* (*www.zerohedge.com*), catch the attention of readers with dramatic headlines (e.g., "If People Stop Believing in Central Banks, All Hell Will Break Loose"). They address a wide range of topics, including economics, geopolitics, commodities, banking, and trading. Multiblogger platforms, such as *Seeking Alpha* (*www.seekingalpha.com*) and *TheStreet* (*www.thestreet.com*), principally feature investment-focused articles. Although some of these multiblogger portals have been criticized for their uneven research quality and potential for author bias, their articles can sometimes be useful supplements to Wall Street analysis. These articles are excellent supplements to Wall Street investment research. Professional money managers, like Josh Brown and Barry Ritholtz, write blogs that help put current business events in a context that is often useful to traders and investors. Other bloggers, like Felix Salmon, are adept at finding interesting and topical business-related subjects and covering them with unique insight.

Zero Hedge: the "Young Iconoclast"

Dan Ivandjiiski might be the most famous financial personality of whom most individual investors have never heard. Ivandjiiski is best known to his readers by his nom de plume, Tyler Durden (this name is borrowed from a fictional character, played by Brad Pitt, in the 1999 cult classic movie hit *Fight Club*). It is believed that other financial writers contribute posts to *Zero Hedge* (*www.zerohedge.com*) under this same pseudonym.

Many individual investors might also be unfamiliar with *Zero Hedge*, the blog associated with Mr. Ivandjiiski. *Zero Hedge* has emerged as a favorite daily read among Wall Street's literati. According to Quantcast, a digital audience-measurement and advertising company, *Zero Hedge* recently attracted about 3.4 million monthly unique visitors. The website has built up an impressive amount of monthly traffic for a publication with the mystique of an underground operation. More mainstream blogging websites, such as *TheStreet* (*www.thestreet.com*) and *Seeking Alpha* (*www.seekingalpha.com*), each attract 8–9 million monthly unique visitors, according to their advertising web pages.

Zero Hedge and its principal contributor with the mysterious pseudonym are not exactly newcomers to the world of financial blogging. In 2009, a *New York Magazine* article, entitled "The Dow Zero Insurgency," shed light on *Zero Hedge*'s little-known principal in a feature article on the burgeoning world of financial blogging. *Zero Hedge* first reared its head in the blogosphere in the early part of that year.

Ivandjiiski became well known after he pounced on a news story about the arrest of Sergey Aleynikov. Mr. Aleynikov was a Goldman Sachs Group trading programmer who had been accused of stealing a proprietary high-frequency trading computer code from his employer. (The basic characteristics of high-frequency trading are discussed in Chapter 9.)

Zero Hedge's coverage of the story became emblematic of its unique brand of investigative journalism—one laced with a deeply cynical distrust of Wall Street. Ivandjiiski became a vocal critic of the perils of high-frequency trading in general, and of The Goldman Sachs Group in particular.

For those unfamiliar with *Fight Club*, from which *Zero Hedge*'s founder drew inspiration for his pen name, the movie follows the life of a mild-mannered automobile company employee, played by Edward Norton. Norton's protagonist befriends the roguish Tyler Durden, an edgy character who assembles a crew of directionless young men into an underground fighting club, bent on pranks of destruction.

Spoiler alert: The movie's protagonist, played by Norton, realizes later in the film that the destructive and fearless Durden is really his own alter ego. The movie then devolves into a series of dark glimpses into the narrator's mental illness, as well as his struggle to derail his nemesis's plan to destroy buildings that house critical financial data.

It is hard to draw a straight line between the dark nihilism of Brad Pitt's Tyler Durden character and the thirty-something-year-old *Zero Hedge* blogger who writes under the character's name. But a dark edginess seems to pervade the pages of *Zero Hedge*, the masthead of which is emblazoned with one of the movie's memorable quotes: "On a long enough timeline, the survival rate for everyone drops to zero."

Zero Hedge is an amalgam of punchy economic analysis, conspiracy theories, and wonky rants about the failings of U.S. political and economic institutions and policies. Recent topics covered by the website include central bank monetary policy, the Cincinnati IRS scandal, U.S. foreign policy and military interventionism, the outlook for gold and precious metals, and other geopolitical worries that bedevil the stock market. Geopolitics also looms large in *Zero Hedge*'s world. Its writers dart back and forth between conventional news coverage and opinion-laden editorials. Readers value the blog's frequent, topical updates and strong point of view. Followers of *Zero Hedge* also praise the author's cerebral brand of cynicism and determination to challenge mainstream views about business, finance, and politics.

Should you read *Zero Hedge*? As with the issue of whom to follow on Twitter, the answer really depends on your personal reading preferences. Many financial advisors and stock investors have bookmarked it (and others like it) and scan it for interesting headlines several times a day.

One advantage of following *Zero Hedge* is that you will become more aware of the topics that are on the minds of those who make a living by buying and selling stocks. Most of Tyler Durden's blog posts are short and to the point. Whether or not you share the author's cynicism, or his stance on economic policy issues, you will likely emerge as a more informed observer of financial markets.

Another key advantage of visiting the *Zero Hedge* website is that its homepage features a list of approximately fifty "*Zero Hedge* Reads." This list of links to other prominent financial blog websites is itself a useful resource (see Exhibit 6). The tendency of bloggers to provide attribution to other writers' articles and to list the names of other influential websites—a feature commonly referred to as a blog roll—can, at times, lead to a lengthy cycle of subreferencing. The inclusion of such blog rolls calls to mind Mindful Money's characterization of the financial blogosphere as being an unwieldy, "carnivalesque conversation."

Exhibit 6: *www.ZeroHedge.com*'s Homepage and List of "Zero Hedge Reads"
Source: *www.ZeroHedge.com*.

Seeking Alpha: the "Blogger's Beehive"

According to its most recent media package, *Seeking Alpha* attracts approximately 8.4 million monthly unique visitors. David Jackson, the website's founder, started the operation in 2004 after a career on both the sell side and buy side of Wall Street. (The sell side refers to brokerage firms that sell securities on a commission basis; the buy side refers to various types of institutions that purchase securities for investment.) *Seeking Alpha*, which is based in New York, has emerged as an important purveyor of news, analysis, and related financial information, including company earnings conference call transcripts.

Why the Name?

The name *Seeking Alpha* provides some insight into the website's emphasis on stock selection and investing ideas. In financial parlance, "alpha" refers to the return of a particular stock in excess of that which would have been predicted by the market's own rate of return, adjusted for the stock's volatility relative to the market. It is this excess return—the return beyond that which can be explained by the market itself—that investors generally endeavor to achieve.

It seems apt to refer to *Seeking Alpha* as the "blogger's beehive" because the website has emerged as an important venue for experienced Wall Street professionals who wish to showcase their written analysis and opinions. *Seeking Alpha* boasts some 7,000 contributing authors and 20,000 commenters. Like other major financial websites, such as *TheStreet*, *Seeking Alpha* syndicates its content to other web-based outlets, which in turn provides its contributors with considerable online exposure and visibility.

Seeking Alpha is also one of the few Internet-based venues that pays its investment writers, albeit at a moderate rate. If a financial writer agrees to contribute content to *Seeking Alpha* on an exclusive basis, he generally gets paid at a rate of $10 per one thousand page views of that content (also referred to as a $10 CPM). While few *Seeking Alpha* contributors would be able to use their writing proceeds to pay for their next trip to the Caribbean, remuneration from the blogger's beehive is actually quite generous compared to other online venues. Yahoo! Voices (*www .voices.yahoo.com*), which features a wide range of contributor content, both business-related and non-business-related, paid its writers at an initial CPM rate of only $1.50. In July 2014, Yahoo! announced that it was shutting down Yahoo! Voices.

Seeking Alpha offers several features that lie outside the scope of its function as a blogging medium but that nevertheless greatly enhance its value, particularly for professional analysts and research-intensive individual investors. One of those useful offerings is the Alerts feature. *Seeking Alpha* visitors can enter a list of stock symbols about which they wish to receive future e-mail Alerts, including notifications about the appearance on the website of related articles and blog posts. Copies of earnings conference call transcripts are also indexed under the stock symbols of public companies.

In what ways are these Alerts useful? For those companies designated on *Seeking Alpha* as Alert stocks, the website's subscribers receive e-mails containing consensus financial projections the day before earnings are reported. They also receive real-time Flash Alerts when the companies' earnings are announced. After the earnings conference calls have been transcribed, Alert subscribers receive e-mails with excerpts from those calls. During the critical earnings-reporting season, these Alerts serve as useful previews and summaries of projected and actual financial results.

Seeking Alpha subscribers can also elect to receive daily e-mails about investing ideas, exchange-traded fund (ETF) strategies, or blog posts on particular sectors. They can also subscribe to any of several daily compendium e-mails. Among the more engaging of those e-mails are *Seeking Alpha*'s "Morning Briefing" that includes popular blog posts and headline articles from the website; and its "Wall Street Breakfast," a series of one-page summaries of top corporate news stories.

The quantity and breadth of information available on the site is one of its notable features. For users who rely more extensively on its non-blog information resources, the fact that the website is the host of multiple blog articles might seem incidental. Although this chapter does not profile other websites that offer content of comparable breadth, two competing financial sites, *TheStreet* and Minyanville (*www.minyanville.com*), offer similar features. They should be considered as alternative resources for individual investors who are interested in websites with a wide range of services.

Felix Salmon: The Buttoned-Down Blogger

The inclusion of Felix Salmon in a chapter about financial blogs is a must—not only because, as a counterpoint to *Zero Hedge*, his blog represents a study in stylistic contrasts, but also because Salmon was engaged in a brief online feud with that rival blog. Like *Zero Hedge*, Salmon takes on the memes of the digital information world. However, he does so with less iconoclasm and more reserve. Salmon's blog posts appeared regularly on Reuters where he was, until recently, a columnist. These blog posts can be found at *blogs.reuters.com/felix-salmon*.

On April 21, 2014, multiple media outlets reported that Salmon was leaving Reuters to pursue another Internet-related opportunity. Several days later, it was revealed that Salmon was joining the cable and digital news network Fusion, as a senior editor. Since arriving at Fusion, Salmon has continued to publish articles on his personal blog, *www.felixsalmon.com*. Some of the posts on this website are proprietary articles, while others are links to opinion-based articles that Salmon had originally published on other media outlets, such as *www.ft.com* and *www .linkedin.com*. In May 2014, Salmon also launched a weekly podcast, *Slate Money*, with several colleagues. Slate (*www.slate.com*) is an online general interest magazine.

Whether it was because of the Reuters masthead, or his more conventional writing style, Salmon's articles resembled those of an established online journalist rather than a roguish "underground" blogger. Felix Salmon's blog posts have included critiques of high-frequency trading, the ridesharing industry, assessments of candidates for the Federal Reserve chairperson, macroeconomic analyses, and brief profiles and senior management appraisals of public companies and hedge funds. Even though he doesn't hesitate to criticize regulators or government leaders, his writing is not as darkly cynical as that which often appears on *Zero Hedge*. Salmon's blog has more of the formality that one would expect of "old-school" print publications such as *The Economist*.

According to his contributor profile on *Seeking Alpha*, which carried his Reuters blog posts, Salmon previously wrote blog pieces for Roubini Global Economics and for Upstart Business Journal. He had worked for *Euromoney* magazine in the UK until 1997, when he relocated to the United States. Nearly 60,000 individuals follow Salmon on *Seeking Alpha*.

If you have a particular interest in financial services or the technology, media, and telecommunications industries— commonly referred to by investors as the TMT sector—then Salmon's articles might be especially helpful to you. Many of the blogger's recent longer written pieces are about companies that fall into those industry categories, including Microsoft, Netflix, Yahoo!, BlackRock, The Goldman Sachs Group, JPMorgan Chase, and MoneyGram International.

On the day of the pricing of the widely anticipated initial public stock offering (IPO) of Twitter, Salmon published a provocative blog article entitled "The Definitive Twitter Value Play." He cited some wide-ranging valuation targets for Twitter that had been featured on several other financial websites and blogs. He then offered a jaundiced view of the financial community's fixation on gauging the worth of the social media company: "*Any* valuation for Twitter is a result of a guess upon guess upon guess."

Salmon advised his readers to "take the amount of money [they] were thinking of investing in Twitter," determine the rate at which they value their own time, and then spend the number of hours, corresponding with the dollar value of that prospective investment, on the Twitter website. In his estimation, "the value [one gets] from being on Twitter . . . will be much greater than the value [one would] ever get from buying" Twitter's stock. By admonishing his readers for being absent from Twitter's website, while, at the same time, dissuading them from investing in the company's shares, Salmon provided a unique perspective on how individual investors should think about this highly publicized equity offering.

Rival bloggers sometimes clash on the blogosphere with just as much drama as the "talking head" journalists who spar on high-profile broadcast news shows such as *Hardball with Chris Matthews*. In a recent blog post entitled "Ten Reasons Barry Ritholtz Is Wrong about Gold," Salmon, in his characteristic cerebral style, took on a Bloomberg (*www.bloomberg.com*) article that had been authored by Ritholtz, a widely followed financial writer and advisor, and the author of the popular *The Big Picture* blog.

Josh Brown: The Merchant of Snark

You might recognize Josh Brown from his frequent appearances on CNBC and other financial news networks. Brown is also the author of *Backstage Wall Street*, a 2012 book that details his observations about the inner workings of the securities industry, including the investment research, stock brokerage, and financial advisory businesses. He is employed as a financial advisor with New York City–based Ritholtz Wealth Management, where Brown is also the firm's chief executive officer.

It is worth noting that one of Josh Brown's colleagues is Barry Ritholtz, the chief investment officer of his namesake firm. Ritholtz's blog articles on *The Big Picture* (*www.ritholtz.com/blog*) are considered by some financial advisors to be a must-read source of commentary and analysis. These blog posts are based on Ritholtz's daily articles that appear on Bloomberg's website.

Josh Brown was labeled "the merchant of snark" by the *New York Times* in its review of his first book, and the nickname seems fitting in many respects. The tone of Brown's writing is often sarcastic. He writes with a more conversational, and less formal, style than Felix Salmon. If Salmon seems to channel the *Economist*'s high-browed didacticism, then Brown's editorial style and tongue-in-cheek one-liners embody the tabloid catchiness of the *New York Post*.

Most of the articles that appear on Brown's blog, *The Reformed Broker* (*www.thereformedbroker.com*), are short and to-the-point. He intersperses comments about popular culture with topical observations and third-party quotations about investing. He has established himself as a tireless curator of other useful, and often amusing, content on the Internet. Among his recurring curated posts are daily clips from CNBC's *Fast Money* and "Hot Links," which features the cartoon image of a sausage link in full stride. "Hot Links" carries one-line summaries and Internet links to "the stuff I'm reading this morning."

Brown has also been known to take on potentially dry subject material with his characteristic wit and sarcasm (e.g., "Fed minuteszzzzzzzzzzz: Ohmygod so boring I fell asleep typing the headline to this post"). Brown's wit and informal style are disarming. The breadth of his commentary and reading interests and the decisive views captured in his blog posts will give you, as an individual investor, some sense of the zeitgeist of the market.

The Reformed Broker has proven to be prescient at certain important junctures. On October 16, 2013, in the immediate wake of the resolution of the U.S. federal government shutdown crisis, Brown wrote a memorable blog post entitled "Rocket Fuel." He enumerated several bullish financial and economic forces that he believed might create a "set-up going into year-end," with all the explosive power of a rocket fuel–powered ignition. The developments he identified included the limited prospects for near-term tapering of the Federal Reserve's quantitative easing program, the benefits of a "highly capitalized" banking system, the post–financial crisis recovery in household net worth, and equity markets' "fair to absurdly cheap valuations."

While his readers might not have agreed with all of the views expressed in that blog post, the article offered a thought-provoking perspective on why the market's near-term outlook should have been viewed as very constructive for investors. As it turned out, the S&P 500 finished 2013 with a 7.4 percent advance from the index's closing level on that mid-October day when feuding factions in the federal government achieved rapprochement. That fact should in no way be interpreted as evidence that *The Reformed Broker*, or any other financial blog, has predictive value. However, observing the market's year-end rally through the prism of that article could certainly have enhanced one's understanding of the economic forces at work.

Reading investment blogs such as *The Reformed Broker* is a useful way to stay on top of the daily "buzz" on Wall Street—absent the iconoclastic edge of *Zero Hedge*, or the more detailed analyses of Felix Salmon. If you would like to bookmark a website that is known for its frequent blog posts, reader accessibility, breadth of subject material, and somewhat lighter-hearted treatment of business events, then Josh Brown's blog might be one worth considering.

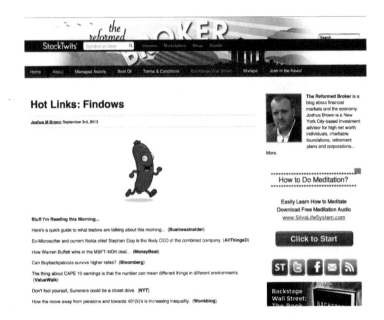

Exhibit 7: The "Hot Links" Page from Josh Brown's
www.TheReformedBroker.com

Source: *www.TheReformedBroker.com.*

The Benefits of Specialized Blogs

While the financial blogs discussed in this chapter can be of enormous value to individuals with a broad range of investing interests, social media users will likely encounter myriad blogs focused on the analysis of specific business subjects and industry sectors. Raymond Deacon, a managing director at Brean Capital and a veteran energy sector stock analyst, relies on several such specialized blogs to supplement his analytical work. Deacon views these blogs as a free source of insight into important financial and operational issues.

One blog that Deacon describes as "extremely useful" is the *Daily Energy Post* blog, published by RBN Energy. RBN Energy is a Texas-based analytics firm that markets advisory and consulting services to corporate clients in the energy sector. Led by former energy trader and analyst Rusty Braziel, the firm's five-person team publishes daily blog articles on a wide range of industry topics. The blog articles are given whimsical titles, laced with puns and the lyrics of classic rock songs. Recent *Daily Energy Post* blog topics have included energy exploration (e.g., oil sands projects); energy production (e.g., gas and natural gas liquids [NGL]); energy transportation logistics (e.g., pipeline projects, crude oil barge activity, and natural gas and liquid petroleum gas [LPG] shipping); commodity price trends (e.g., crude oil and natural gas prices); and petrochemical manufacturing inputs.

Deacon cites an important example of how the *Daily Energy Post* had alerted him to a nonconsensus viewpoint about an industry development. In a series of articles, the *Daily Energy Post* focused on the recoverable NGL market. The blog's author concluded that the pipeline transportation capacity being built for the industry would be adequate to move natural gas from the Marcellus Shale in the Appalachian Basin to customers in other regions of the country. That conclusion, which turned out to be correct, defied prevailing concerns about the adequacy of NGL transportation infrastructure.

A Caveat about Blog Author Authenticity and Motivation

The websites discussed in this chapter are widely read, and they are respected for their editorial and analytical content. However, you should be aware that the motivations of blog writers are not always consistent with the editorial standards of their hosting websites. *Seeking Alpha* allows its research authors to publish articles under aliases. In February 2014, *Seeking Alpha* removed from its website two articles, both of which had been written by a single individual who was using two different pseudonyms. Both of the articles contained favorable views about the stock of Galena Biopharma, a manufacturer of biopharmaceutical products.

The Galena Biopharma articles became the subject of considerable controversy when a columnist at *TheStreet* reported, on February 12, 2014, that Galena Biopharma had been linked "to a stock-promotions firm which wrote and published the articles on *Seeking Alpha*." According to *TheStreet*, "the articles were part of a broader, coordinated 'brand' awareness campaign designed to boost Galena's stock price." *TheStreet*'s article revealed further that "Galena [had] paid $50,000 to a subsidiary of The DreamTeam Group for 240 days of 'advertising, branding, marketing, and investor relations and social media services.'"

As of the writing of this book, the management team of Galena Biopharma has not commented on the controversy surrounding the company's stock. However, dramatic swings in Galena Biopharma's share price have held the attention of traders. The company's stock rose from $2.28 on September 30, 2013, to a peak price of $7.48 on January 16, 2014. As of April 15, 2014, against the backdrop of the promotion controversy, the stock had slid to $1.74. By June 23, 2014, it had recovered to $3.13.

The recent events involving *Seeking Alpha* echoed an earlier incident involving seven biopharmaceutical company stocks, including Galena Biopharma. In January 2013, *TheStreet* reported that *Seeking Alpha* had removed five articles about these biopharmaceutical stocks from its website. While the articles had been authored under three different pseudonyms, *Seeking Alpha* management learned that a single individual had written all of them.

For its part, *Seeking Alpha* has defended its policy of editorial anonymity. During a February 2014 interview with *Barron's*,

Seeking Alpha's editor-in-chief stated that "a policy of disallowing anonymity would give [*Seeking Alpha* articles] a bias to the bull side." Other observers of *Seeking Alpha*'s policy of permitting its contributors to publish articles using pseudonyms believe that "anonymity has given *Seeking Alpha* writers the freedom to expose wrongdoing in the corporate world without fear of retribution."

Instances of blog author bias and inauthenticity are not unique to *Seeking Alpha*. Readers of all stock commentary, sourced from both offline and online channels, need to be aware of the potential motives underlying the content of investment articles. In the same sense, the advantages of using Twitter, which are discussed at length in Chapter 2, must be weighed against the risks associated with the unknown identities of many tweeters. The potential risks of taking editorial content at "face value" are amplified when articles are published under the veil of anonymity that is permitted by some editorial platforms.

Key Takeaways from Chapter Three

- Blogs are similar to traditional journalists' articles, but also feature reader comments and social media voting widgets.
- *Zero Hedge* is a prolific blog that discusses financial and economic developments with a cynical, sometimes iconoclastic, viewpoint.
- *Seeking Alpha* is a "beehive" of activity for some 7,000 contributing blog authors, many of whom are investment professionals.
- *The Reformed Broker* author Josh Brown and his colleague, *The Big Picture* author Barry Ritholtz, cover a wide range of investment topics with wit and humor.
- Blog readers must remain aware of the potential motivations of article contributors, including those individuals who publish pseudonymously.

CHAPTER FOUR

Feeding on RSS Feeds

The proliferation of investment blogs, online periodicals, and social media websites has spawned an enormous amount of reading material that allows you to stay abreast of business news and financial market developments. Fortunately, the burgeoning world of social media has also made available powerful Internet-based resources that can enable you to identify and organize new editorial content. This chapter will introduce you to the features of RSS readers, and then explain the related benefits of using social media dashboard services and news-reading applications. These tools help you find new online content quickly, and prioritize that content, based on its subject matter and relevance.

An Introduction to RSS Feeds

If you are new to the world of social media and its cryptic iconography, you might not be quite sure what to make of the RSS icon. This symbol, a small orange square with broadcast waves emanating from the top right corner, is the universal symbol for an RSS link (RSS stands for "rich site summary," or more commonly "really simple syndication"). If that explanation is not sufficiently illuminating to you, you are not alone. Many investors are unfamiliar with RSS feeds, and many others don't use them even if they are familiar with the term.

"Really simple syndication" is an online tool that enables organizations to "syndicate" their content by making it available to visitors who subscribe to their RSS feed. Companies and media outlets use this powerful tool to build an audience of loyal followers. RSS feeds are also a useful resource for website visitors and investors who can elect to subscribe to the feeds of specific companies or news organizations. The advantage of subscribing to RSS feeds is that all of your news and media alerts are consolidated into a single area on your computer.

The first step in obtaining access to RSS feeds is to download an RSS reader. RSS readers function as aggregators of content from the websites users visit frequently. There are many types of RSS readers, including a variety of free services. To start, I recommend you consider Feedreader. This is free software that you can download and use to obtain access to RSS feeds from a variety of publications and companies.

Some observers of the social web might characterize RSS feeds as an outdated medium. Internet users are increasingly relying on Twitter, Facebook, LinkedIn, Google+, and other social media applications described in this book to obtain access to news stories. However, using RSS feeds offers you certain advantages in the crowded world of social media because they enable you, as a subscriber, to put limits on the aggregated content and information that interests you.

How is the source-specific aggregation capability of an RSS reader an advantage to you? One of the defining, and sometimes most frustrating, characteristics of Twitter is its unfiltered nature. Those individuals and organizations that you choose to follow on Twitter are likely to tweet about a wide range of subjects, and some of those topics may be of limited interest to you. In a similar vein, conducting hashtag-based searches on Twitter can yield a wide swath of results.

For example, if you were to conduct a Twitter-based search using the hashtag "#Facebook," you are likely to encounter many different types of references to Facebook, including Facebook's societal impact, Facebook-related business and investment news, and observations about user experiences on Facebook—material that is most likely of limited value from an investing point of view. In contrast, by subscribing to the RSS feed on Facebook's Investor Relations web page, you can hone in on news and investor-related content provided by the company.

Many professional research analysts use RSS readers to compile and filter news stories related to the companies and industries they follow. For example, some industry analysts subscribe to the RSS feeds of trade publications, as well as regional newspapers associated with geographic regions in which the publicly traded stocks they follow have operating facilities. RSS readers also enable users to retrieve news stories related to specific search terms. This filtering capability enables RSS subscribers to create more narrowly defined news feeds that are based on industry-related keywords and topics.

The Efficiency of News Feeds

As a gaming industry analyst, I regularly monitor regulatory activity and political developments in states that permit casino wagering. One of my routine research steps involves tracking news stories in cities and states where gaming properties are located, or where they are being developed. Using an RSS reader, I can create an alphabetized list of RSS links to a variety of daily newspaper business sections that interest me. These newspapers routinely feature information about local business and political developments related to the operation or expansion of gaming facilities.

For example, in order to more closely track political activity in Springfield, Massachusetts, where several casino companies have targeted future resort developments, I added the RSS link from the business news page of MassLive, which is the website of the *Republican*, a newspaper based in Springfield, Massachusetts. In June 2014, the Massachusetts Gaming Commission awarded a gaming license to MGM Springfield. The addition of that RSS link is shown at the top of Exhibit 8, right below the field labeled, "add feed."

After I added the MassLive.com RSS link, my RSS reader application began to carry updated business news headlines from the *www.masslive.com* website. By obtaining access to the RSS feed of MassLive.com, I have been able to track business news stories from that source without ever having to visit that website.

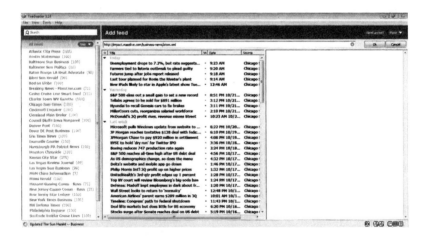

Exhibit 8: Feedreader Screen: Adding a News Feed
Source: Brian Egger's copy of Feedreader 3.14.

WHAT IS AN XML FILE?

Newcomers to RSS readers might not recognize the "atom.xml" suffix at the end of the RSS link, shown in the "Add feed" field in Exhibit 8. XML stands for "extensible markup language," which is similar to the more commonly used HTML (hypertext markup language). XML is a computer language that enables different computer systems to share formats and data. "Atom" is the name of a popular XML-based document format used to work with RSS feeds.

Using Smartfeed

After gathering a collection of RSS feeds you can use a Feedreader feature called "Smartfeed" to organize news items in ways that are useful to you. Using the Smartfeed application of Feedreader (*www.feedreader.com*) enables you to create a subset of news stories from the newspaper business sections that are pertinent to your sector focus. In order to take advantage of the filtering capacity of Feedreader's Smartfeed tool, you must include a series of sorting rules that instruct Feedreader to select relevant stories and store them in a Smartfeed folder. The top of the screenshot in Exhibit 9 illustrates how these search criteria can be put into action.

Using Smartfeed, for example, I listed a series of keywords that are relevant to my research work on the gaming sector, such as "casino," "gaming," and "racetrack." The search rules I created helped to identify news articles that contained those gaming-related words in either the title or the main body. Other search-related words are hidden below the bottom of the scroll-down screen at the top of the exhibit.

Using those keywords, Feedreader's Smartfeed application calls up a series of newspaper articles drawn from all of my RSS-linked websites shown on the left-hand column of Exhibit 9. (These articles were selected by the Feedreader algorithm because they contain the keywords that I had used to populate the filtering application on the top of the exhibit.) I can also update my Smartfeed feature with new criteria that I specify, such as the inclusion or exclusion of other key-words. The updated Smartfeed then yields a "smarter" list of news articles that are more likely to contain information pertaining to my area of research focus. It is my hope that even this brief introduction to RSS feeds illustrates how useful they can be as time-saving and efficiency-maximizing devices for you as an investor.

Exhibit 9: Feedreader Screen: Editing the "Smartfeed"
Source: Brian Egger's copy of Feedreader 3.14.

Using RSS Feeds to Track Companies

RSS feeds supplied by company investor relations departments provide a useful way to monitor corporate news and announce-ments. The screenshot in Exhibit 10 features the main Investor

Relations page of Penn National Gaming Inc., a major casino operator. In order to subscribe to one of Penn National Gaming Inc.'s RSS feeds, you need only click the "RSS Feeds" icon in the Investor Relations box that appears on the bottom right corner of the exhibit. Clicking an RSS icon directs you to another web page that contains three RSS subscription links. There you are likely to encounter choices such as "All News Releases," "All Calendar Events," or "All SEC Filings." By selecting the "All News Releases" RSS icon, for example, and subscribing to a corporate RSS feed, alerts about future company news releases will automatically appear in your RSS reader. By including links to company news releases or investor relations events in an RSS reader, you can customize a Smartfeed RSS folder to include both relevant newspaper articles and company-issued announcements.

Exhibit 10: Penn National Gaming, Inc. Investor Relations Page
Source: *http://phx.corporate-ir.net/phoenix.zhtml?c=120420&p=irol-irhome.*

RSS Feeds Simplify the Tracking
of Financial Bloggers

As a stock market investor, you would do well to utilize several techniques that enable you to filter multiple articles in an efficient manner. These shortcuts can help you organize what could otherwise be an overwhelming volume of blog headlines and news articles.

One of those techniques involves bookmarking websites on your web browser, so you can readily access them with a single touch. Many market professionals have developed a daily reading regimen in which they hop from website to website to get a quick overview of news and blog articles. After completing this overview, they then decide which items they want to read in greater depth. I have streamlined my own blog-reading efforts by configuring an RSS reader with the feeds of six major bloggers. Three of those blogs—*Zero Hedge*, Felix Salmon, and *The Reformed Broker*—are discussed in detail in Chapter 3.

There are a number of free RSS apps available for iPhone and iPad users, and the Newsify (*www.newsify.co*) app is a great addition to any investor's toolbox. This app renders a newspaper-like article list that lays out the most recent articles from a preselected list of blogs. Adding a new blog source to your Newsify feed is as simple as hitting a "+" button and then typing the name of a particular blog in a search box.

Using Newsify is fairly intuitive. The application lists each blog's RSS feed separately, creating a list of bookmarks that is similar to those you might maintain on a web browser. Newsify also features menu choices such as "All Items" and "Unread Items" that enable you to view an aggregated list of headlines and synopses from all of the blogs for which you've subscribed to an RSS feed. You can simply pull down on the screen to refresh the article list, and then scroll through articles. You can also click through a headline on Newsify to get access to the source article on its host website.

If you plan to include blog-reading as one of your strategies for staying on top of your investments (and I strongly recommend you do), or wish to receive a wide range of editorial views on pertinent business topics, then you will likely find an RSS reader to be an indispensable tool. This is true even if you prefer to limit your business reading to a narrow group of journalists and bloggers. Given that there are a number of free apps available to tablet and smartphone users, as well as free software packages available for desktop aficionados, there is no reason not to give them a try.

Social Media Dashboard Services

Social media dashboard services are software applications that enable users to manage their message feeds from multiple social media accounts and to customize a series of "streams" that provide updates from those accounts. Although these services differ from RSS readers, their ability to funnel messages from multiple online sources through a single portal resembles the way in which RSS readers are used. Similarly, some of these dashboard services have the ability to incorporate RSS feeds, as well as social media message streams.

One of these social media dashboard services, TweetDeck (*www.tweetdeck.com*), was acquired by Twitter in 2011. Because there is no longer an iPad app available for TweetDeck, and because TweetDeck has more recently focused on desktop portal applications, I suggest you instead opt to use a competing service called Hootsuite (*www.hootsuite.com*). Hootsuite is a privately owned company based in Vancouver, Canada, and recently had 7 million registered users.

> **WHAT'S IN A NAME?**
>
> Originally named Brightkit, the company was rebranded into Hootsuite by a customer, who suggested the catchy name, in response to a company-sponsored naming contest. The new name pairs convincingly with the image of an owl that is used as the company's logo.

Hootsuite

Hootsuite operates by connecting with Facebook, Twitter, or LinkedIn, as well as Google+. The free, basic version of Hootsuite allows users to integrate as many as five different social media accounts. However, you could use the service to organize feeds from your Twitter and LinkedIn business accounts only. The professional version of the software, which costs $8.99 per month, accommodates as many as fifty social media accounts, as well as an unlimited number of RSS feeds and more advanced message archiving and security features.

Hootsuite's uses for Twitter include the ability to schedule and send future tweets and to track, in separate streams, incoming tweets, direct messages, and "mentions" from other Twitter users. ("Mentions" occur when other Twitter users make reference to your past tweets in their own tweets.) Hootsuite's search capabilities are particularly well suited to stock and financial research. You can set up permanent streams based on those searches, or for keywords and phrases. Monitoring search-based streams from multiple social media sources enables you to stay abreast of developments and insights that you might not find on conventional business media websites.

On the Twitter tab of my Hootsuite app, I have set up searches for gaming and leisure-related phrases, such as "MGM National Harbor" and "cruise bookings." I have specified the keyword, "RevPAR," which stands for "revenue per available room," an important operating metric in the hospitality industry. I have also added a separate stream based on the keyword "$RCL," which is the stock symbol cashtag for Royal Caribbean Cruises. In addition to these search term–related streams, I have added a stream on my Hootsuite app for the RSS feed of the *Las Vegas Review-Journal*, an important source of gaming-related news.

Of course, I could always use the search window on Twitter to find messages relevant to search terms like "RevPAR" and "$RCL," but using Hootsuite to monitor these terms offers me the convenience of rendering parallel columns of vertical streams on the same computer screen. On my tablet, I am able to monitor recent tweets under the column headings "MGM National Harbor," "cruise bookings," "RevPAR," and "$RCL." In order to refresh any of these streams with the most recent messages, I simply swipe my finger downward on the column heading for the appropriate search term. This is a much more efficient and easier searching procedure than routinely reentering these search terms in a Twitter search box.

Social News-Reading Applications

You should become familiar with some of the related social media services that help aggregate your online news feeds, including those related to business and investing. These applications are often referred to as "social news-reading apps" or as "new aggregating apps." While different from RSS readers, these software services possess similar aggregation capabilities. Among the best known of these mobile device–focused news-reading services are LinkedIn's Pulse app, Zite, Flipboard, and Facebook's Paper app.

In April 2013, LinkedIn, the professional networking website operator, acquired a news-aggregating software application called Pulse (*www.pulse.me*). At the time of its acquisition, Pulse had 30 million members. This service enables users to create personalized news feeds. LinkedIn users can obtain access to Pulse via the "Interests" pull-down menu on the main LinkedIn user interface, or they can download a free app on their mobile device and use Pulse as a stand-alone service. The professional interest group features of LinkedIn are described at some length in Chapter 5.

Users of Pulse can elect to follow a series of "channels" that include topics ranging from "big data" to "finance and banking." The experience of following channels on LinkedIn's Pulse app is similar to that of subscribing to topic-specific boards on the social bookmarking website Pinterest (described in Chapter 8). For example, by searching under the term "investing" on Pulse, you can find channels for a number of popular financial websites and blogs that include *TheStreet*, The Motley Fool (*www.themotleyfool.com*), *Forbes* (*www.forbes.com*), and *Businessweek* (*www.businessweek.com*).

For its part, Zite (*www.zite.com*) functions as a personalized magazine for tablet and smartphone devices. Zite had been owned by CNN, but was sold to Flipboard, another news-reading app operator.

Flipboard (*www.flipboard.com*), while originally introduced in late 2010, has undergone a series of product upgrades. Flipboard is a news-reading app that enables you to subscribe to a series of news sections that include "Technology," "Design," "Style," and "Photography." You can add a section subscription, such as "Business," to a Flipboard account. Within the "Business" section you can "flip" through pages using a process that simulates reading a book. By clicking a "+" button you can flip your favorite stories, transferring them to a customized magazine that you can access later within a separate booklet. You can also bookmark news stories or copy article URL links into Twitter messages or e-mails. Flipboard, like other news-reading apps discussed in this chapter, relies on algorithms and social network feeds to present stories.

In February 2014, Facebook introduced a news-reading mobile application called Paper (*www.facebook.com/paper*). The Paper app presents twenty topical sections, with your own Facebook News Feed included as a default section. Users can choose from among sections labeled "Headlines," "PopLife," "Flavor," "Tech," and "Enterprise." Using your tablet, you can swipe any of these topical sections into a customized Paper. In order to optimize your news-reading experience, you may wish to select business-related Facebook Paper categories, such as "Enterprise," which features "news and insights about companies, global markets and savvy investing"; and "Tech," which facilitates "understanding today's startups and tomorrow's innovators." After you've selected these sections, you can move horizontally between them.

Each Paper section reveals a series of vertical panels that contain news stories from various mainstream and trade-oriented media sources. The Paper app also enables you to post updates to your status, photos, and other materials to Facebook. After identifying an important news story, you can select it and reveal a full-screen summary card for that story, and then click or swipe it a second time to render the full story in its original media source. The app's features are easy to use. According to a *Wall Street Journal* review of Paper, the new Facebook utility operates under the assumption that "Facebook's computer-assisted editors are probably better than your friends at selecting stories." Some technology journalists have speculated that Paper's effectiveness as a newsreader could cannibalize the Facebook website and become the Facebook of the future.

While LinkedIn's Pulse presents an interesting way to organize your news feeds, you may find it sufficient to rely on RSS readers and social media dashboard services. However, some newer news-reading apps, such as the most recent version of Flipboard and Facebook's Paper, simplify and refine the news-reading experience, and do so in interesting ways. Flipboard and Paper, while still evolving as mobile apps, can nonetheless serve as useful social media alternatives to RSS readers.

Key Takeaways from Chapter Four

- The advantage of subscribing to RSS feeds is that all of your news and media alerts are consolidated in a single area on your computer.
- Many analysts use RSS readers to compile and filter news stories related to the companies and industries they follow.
- Smartfeeds enable users of RSS readers to create subsets of news stories, identified by using a series of keywords that are pertinent to their research focus.
- RSS feeds maintained by company investor relations officers and financial bloggers are another useful way to organize and monitor corporate news and editorials.
- Social media management dashboards, such as Hootsuite, enable you to manage and monitor "streams" of messages from multiple social media accounts.
- Recently introduced news-reading applications, such as Flipboard and Facebook's Paper, provide alternative ways for you to organize and prioritize news stories.

CHAPTER FIVE

Crowdsourced and Curated Websites

One of the exciting recent developments in social media has been the popularization of so-called "crowdsourced" websites. These websites gather investment opinions and financial estimates from across the web and curate them by filtering, organizing, and presenting them to users. In this chapter, we'll talk about the philosophical underpinnings of crowdsourced investing, a practice that traces its intellectual roots to the behavioral finance concept known as the "wisdom of crowds." We'll then discuss the essential features of several popular crowdsourced finance and investing websites, including StockTwits, Estimize, and SumZero. We'll also consider the prescient analytical work of a widely followed StockTwits contributor, and his impact on other investors, as an example of how you can benefit from using crowdsourced investment platforms. If you want to get smarter about investing by listening to other smart investors, an awareness of these resources can be extremely valuable. So read on, and tap into "the wisdom of crowds!"

Stock Market Wisdom from a "Hill of Beans"?

Six years ago, while teaching a securities analysis course at Columbia Business School, I introduced MBA students to the concept of the "wisdom of crowds" by asking them to guess the number of jelly beans in a glass jar. I borrowed this instructive exercise from Michael Mauboussin, a Columbia Business School professor, prominent author, and managing director of global investment strategies at Credit Suisse. Mauboussin cites a 1987 *Financial Analysts Journal* article by Jack Treynor, a well-known financial economist and investment advisor, as the inspiration for his experiment.

In the experiment, the student in the class who submits the most accurate guess regarding the number of beans in the jar receives a small cash reward, while the least accurate guesser is assigned a small penalty. Of the seventy-three students in Mauboussin's 2007 securities analysis class, only two individuals submitted a guess that turned out to be more accurate than the class's average estimate. In my smaller class of thirty students, only two participants provided a guess that was closer to the actual bean count of 825 than the average conjecture of 891 beans. In each case, the class's consensus estimate was more accurate than that of nearly all individual participants.

This example of the predictive "wisdom of crowds" requires three preconditions in order to function properly. First, individual participants have to think differently, because they have different perspectives and models. Second, there must be a way to bring together the group's viewpoints. Finally, individuals must be rewarded for being correct and penalized for being wrong. A small cash reward is a sufficient incentive for students participating in the jelly bean jar experiment.

Professor Mauboussin and others have cited the wisdom of crowds as a plausible explanation for the efficiency of capital markets. As defined by Investopedia (*www.investopedia.com*), the efficient market hypothesis holds that stock prices incorporate all available information. According to this framework, it is very difficult to "beat the market" because stocks have already discounted all information held by "the crowd." The wisdom-of-crowds framework has also provided an intellectual backdrop for the launch of new financial tools that rely on crowdsourced inputs. These tools tap into the power of today's social media–driven "phooey-on-the-experts" mindset, and rely on input from large groups of individuals.

The ascension of crowdsourced decision-making parallels other developments in the corporate world. Business and financial leaders who had based their professional authority on conventional credentials, such as top-school MBA degrees, have been supplanted by new experts that include upstart hedge fund managers and bloggers. This phenomenon echoes a similar trend in popular culture. Established and skilled dancers, musicians, and fashion experts are being displaced by reality television contest winners who spring from obscurity overnight.

StockTwits: More than Just Cashtags

StockTwits (*www.stocktwits.com*) was cofounded in 2008 by a native Torontonian and hedge fund manager named Howard Lindzon. The website's early use of the cashtag search convention (i.e., "$[stock symbol]") has become a defining feature of social finance—one that Twitter itself officially adopted in 2012. The cashtag convention, as conceived by StockTwits, organizes streams of information about stocks and financial markets that is sourced from users of StockTwits and other social media websites.

The look and feel of the StockTwits dashboard resembles that of a trading chat room or a financial website message board.

StockTwits can be integrated with your Facebook, Twitter, and LinkedIn accounts, so that your posts automatically appear on your account page of those other social media platforms.

While StockTwits can be a useful tool for a wide range of users, the rapidly flowing stream of messages yielded by the platform is a terrific tool for active traders and individuals who live and breathe stocks. If you are looking for a rapidly moving conveyor belt of stock and market news, observations, and opinions, then StockTwits might be for you.

For those individuals who have a more narrowly defined interest in the stock market, the general "Equities" stream of StockTwits might seem like information overload. New comments on a wide range of stocks scroll down the screen at the speed of approximately forty-five or fifty message posts per minute. Unlike Twitter, the users of which must pull down the Home screen to render up-to-date tweets, StockTwits has a default feature that displays new messages in a continuous, real-time stream.

In order to navigate the information flows on StockTwits, you may want to follow one of several more narrowly filtered streams. This is the realm in which StockTwits's curating role becomes vital. Some of the site's actively curated message-viewing options will allow you to follow the messages produced by "suggested" users and review the messages that pertain to "trending" stocks—those that appear with a high degree of frequency on the system (see Exhibit 11).

Alternatively, StockTwits visitors with an affinity for technical analysis might prefer to track a stream of all trading charts produced by the user community. Specialized streams are also available for those of you who have a particular interest in trading currencies or futures.

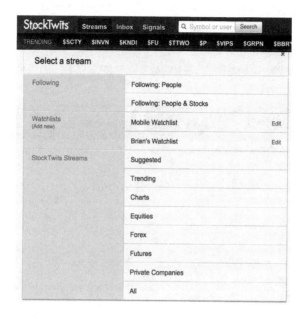

Exhibit 11: *www.StockTwits.com* Message Stream Menu
Source: *www.StockTwits.com.*

Some investors have a particular interest in the outlook for securities of companies that operate in a specific industry. If you are a sector-focused analyst, you can choose to narrow your research focus by creating a stock-specific personal "watchlist" on StockTwits. For example, by selecting the "Brian's Watchlist" stream on my StockTwits account, I am able to monitor all user message posts that pertain to the ten gaming and travel stocks that I follow most closely. "Brian's Watchlist," a snapshot of which appears in Exhibit 12, illustrates the range of message types that are typically featured in a customized StockTwits stream. The posts on this watchlist usually include a potpourri of company news announcements, links to relevant financial blog articles, updates about sell-side analyst rating and price target changes, and snippets of bullish or bearish user views about the trading outlook for stocks. Even if you aren't a market junkie, your ability to filter StockTwits message streams in this manner is useful if you want to be immersed in the flow of news and opinions about stocks that belong to a subset of companies.

Exhibit 12: BreakingCall's "Watchlist" Stream on *www.StockTwits.com*
Source: *www.StockTwits.com.*

StockTwits has important graphical features for investors who wish to become better informed about the implications of messages submitted by StockTwits users who follow a particular stock. The message stream associated with a stock is accompanied by a default version of a conventional stock price chart. Users of StockTwits can also choose to review revealing graphical representations of community message activity by clicking other graphing options: "Message Volume" and "Sentiment." These charting features unveil the potential range of insights you can obtain by participating in a crowdsourced stock commentary community.

The Message Volume chart, which is activated by clicking the "Message Volume" tab above the charting area of your StockTwits screen, depicts a time series of the volume of message posts about a stock that have been submitted by StockTwits members. According to the site, this chart illustrates the "seven-day StockTwits volume for an individual stock" and "gives . . . a good gauge of social momentum."

The Sentiment chart, which you can activate by clicking the "Sentiment" tab above the charting area, reveals "the percentage breakdown in bullish and bearish sentiment shared by StockTwits users over time. It is calculated on a rolling, seven-day basis." Every StockTwits user who elects to share an idea about a particular stock has the option of choosing between a green-shaded bull indicator and a red-shaded bear indicator. StockTwits contributors may opt to enter a message post without selecting either of these two sentiment indicators.

Individual investors might prefer instead to follow the message posts of particular StockTwits contributors whose opinions they value, regardless of the stocks being discussed. If you are one of those investors, you can opt to follow a particular group of people whom you regard as important opinion leaders. By linking your StockTwits account with your Twitter account, you can track message posts delivered by the same individuals you already follow on Twitter. This filtering functionality—the ability to tap into one or more "streams" of carefully curated message posts—distinguishes the StockTwits messaging service from the message boards of other financial websites where a "free-for-all" deluge of posts is the norm.

StockTwits also allows its users to obtain a high-level view of activity in the stock market. This important feature, called a "Social Heatmap," provides an activity gauge that is determined by the frequency and volume of social media messages being generated by StockTwits users, as well as the direction of stock price movements. In technology parlance, a heatmap is a graphical representation of data. The StockTwits Heatmap looks like a jigsaw puzzle with myriad color-coded pieces that appear in quadrants, representing broad industry sectors: Basic Materials, Consumer Goods, Financials, Healthcare, Services, and Technology. The pieces of the puzzle alternately appear as shades of red, which signifies a downward trading move; or green, which indicates an upward stock price move. The size of each puzzle piece is indicative of "social volume," or the quantity of user messages generated about a particular sector, during a given timeframe.

As a StockTwits user, you can obtain additional insight into market trading sentiment for individual stocks by clicking on the name of a particular sector in the Heatmap. Exhibit 13 features a technology sector Heatmap graphic. The grid represents the direction of stock price moves, as well as the volume of social media message activity, generated during the preceding six hours. Not surprisingly, the cashtag symbol for Apple Inc., the U.S. technology company with the largest market capitalization as of this writing, is currently associated with the largest puzzle piece in the technology Heatmap on StockTwits.

StockTwits's Signals tool and its Heatmap product are features that will likely appeal to individual investors with an active trading mindset: those who wish to gauge the tone and feel of the overall market trading environment. The availability of these signaling tools is also a feature that distinguishes StockTwits from major financial news websites, such as Yahoo! Finance (*www.finance.yahoo.com*) and Google Finance (*www.google.com/finance*). These popular financial websites track the direction of stock price moves but don't directly provide the added context of market sentiment, as measured by social media message activity.

As will be discussed in Chapter 6, Yahoo! recently introduced a Market Pulse feature that enables its financial website visitors to view a stream of message updates from StockTwits, as well as another crowdsourcing website, Covestor (*www.covestor.com*).

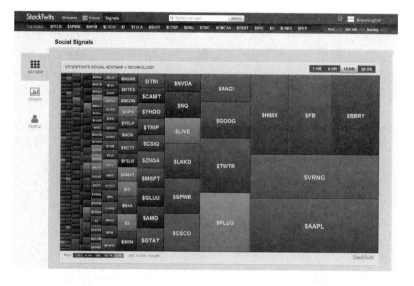

Exhibit 13: StockTwits Heatmap for Technology Sector
Source: *www.StockTwits.com* (as of September 19, 2013).

As a business enterprise, StockTwits has undertaken new ways to market its services to the investment community. Like Twitter, StockTwits sells its data feed to media outlets, such as Bloomberg, Yahoo!, and Reuters. StockTwits has also expanded the relevance of its platform by marketing investor relations services to corporations. Using StockTwits Investor Communications Solutions, investor relations officers at public companies can create and manage an "official" StockTwits web page that streams investor-oriented company announcements and answers to conference call questions alongside the commentary supplied by investors.

The adoption of StockTwits and other social media platforms by corporate investor relations officers is an important development. It reflects a growing awareness on the part of the managers of publicly traded companies that their shareholders increasingly rely on social media to obtain investment-related information. According to a 2013 study by the National Investor Relations Institute, approximately half of all professional investors read blogs and incorporate social media in their investment process. Moreover, about 60 percent of all financial bloggers rely on Twitter as their primary news source.

CORPORATE TWITTER ACCOUNTS

According to Q4 Web Systems, a developer of investor relations websites, the vast majority of publicly traded companies have a Twitter account. About 72 percent of those Twitter-using companies employ that social media application to distribute investor relations material. Of the 890 publicly traded companies included in the Q4 Web Systems study, 66 percent were reported to have a presence on StockTwits. These statistics underscore the extent to which the executives of major corporations, who are increasingly aware of the information consumption preferences of their stakeholders, are adopting social media platforms as a means of distributing financial news.

StockTwits Goes to College

As StockTwits has grown in popularity, the website has gained the attention of university finance scholars who study the predictive relevance of social media messages. In one such study, prepared in 2013 by Chris Loughlin and Erik Harnisch, the authors examined how well StockTwits predicts daily stock returns. Examining 19,000 StockTwits messages that had been originated during the first quarter of 2013, Loughlin and Harnisch concluded that the bull and bear indicators on the StockTwits website are significant predictors of the future stock market returns of Apple, Google, and Microsoft.

To be fair, another academic study, also completed in 2013, contradicted the conclusions of the paper published by Loughlin and Harnisch. The second study found no evidence that Stock-Twits sentiment indicators predict future stock returns. However, the authors of the second study, which was published in the journal *Progress in Artificial Intelligence*, did conclude that the volume of StockTwits message posts helps forecast stock trading volumes, a key gauge of market liquidity.

A Powerful Example of the StockTwits Community at Work

Joe Tranfo, a private investor and avid StockTwits fan, provides a great example of how the crowdsourced financial network has made him a better investor. Tranfo's StockTwits messages acknowledge the valuable insights he has gained from another stock investor, Michael Bigger, who has about 18,000 followers on the website. Bigger's investment in, and analysis of, a fuel cell technology company called Plug Power have been closely followed by Tranfo and others on the StockTwits platform.

In May 2013, when Plug Power's stock was trading at $0.28, Bigger articulated his investment thesis for the company on his blog. Plug Power manufactures hydrogen-powered fuel cells that function as a clean-energy alternative to batteries in the forklifts used in distribution and assembly facilities. Bigger's subsequent writing on Plug Power took the form of some fifty StockTwits messages, diligently logged over a period of nine months. Bigger's unfolding series of messages created a powerful narrative. He recounted the findings of his channel checks, including the potential revenue opportunities represented by prospective orders from large customers, including Walmart and Kroger, should those retailers deploy Plug Power's fuel cells at multiple distribution centers.

Bigger's StockTwits message posts included an assertion that "Plug Power is the best public company investment opportunity I have ever seen in my life," coupled with a caveat that the company is "highly distressed with high probability it goes to zero." In a September 2013 blog post, Bigger disclosed that his firm, Bigger Capital, owned 3 percent of Plug Power, even as he cautioned his readers that "Plug Power is a highly distressed situation . . . not suitable for the majority of investors."

Plug Power's "multisite" fuel cell deals eventually created enough of a business pipeline for the company to convince investors of its long-term viability. As of late-June 2014, the stock was trading at approximately $4.75. Describing his experience on StockTwits, Joe Tranfo expressed "kudos to Mike [Bigger] for his work and to . . . the StockTwits platform, which is where I was first exposed to Mike's writings." In Tranfo's view, Bigger's early writings on Plug Power, when the company had appeared financially distressed, have been "vindicated" by its later successes. In a February 2014 blog post, Howard Lindzon, the cofounder of StockTwits, also gave Bigger a "standing ovation" for his notable work on Plug Power.

A Prominent Financial Advisor Extols the Value of StockTwits

You might assume that high-profile investment advisors, with many information sources and market contacts at their disposal, would have less of a need to follow the discussion streams found on free-access crowdsourcing websites such as StockTwits. It might therefore come as a surprise that one of StockTwits's most effusive advocates is Josh Brown, the CEO of Ritholtz Wealth

Management. *The Reformed Broker*, Brown's widely followed blog, is profiled in Chapter 3.

Brown began participating in StockTwits on a regular basis in 2010. He followed "the 'suggested' stream on StockTwits. Over the course of four years, [he] received an education on trading that . . . helped [him] learn and navigate various market conditions." Brown embraces the instructional value of the website, noting that "if you educate yourself with the resources available on StockTwits, you can cut down the amount of mistakes, learn faster . . . and [achieve] your investing and trading goals."

Brown admires the seasoned traders whom he regards as mentors in the practice of "trend-trading." This is defined in Investopedia (*www.investopedia.com*) as a "strategy that attempts to capture gains through the analysis of an asset's momentum in a particular direction." Among the traders who have influenced Brown's investing style are Howard Lindzon and Greg Harmon, the founder of Dragonfly Capital Management. Harmon focuses on technical analysis and trading strategies involving common stocks and stock options. Lindzon and Harmon have approximately 73,000 followers and 54,000 followers, respectively, on StockTwits.

Estimize: Another Way to Get Market Wise

Estimize (*www.estimize.com*) is a prominent example of a crowd-sourced investment platform with a growing institutional audience. The New York–based company, which began operations in 2011, culls earnings estimates from about 4,700 buy-side analysts, sell-side analysts, portfolio managers, and hedge funds. According to Estimize, its crowdsourced forecasts on some 900 stocks have beaten consensus sell-side estimates between 67 percent and 77 percent of the time, depending on the number of analysts who contribute estimates for a particular company. (A larger number of estimate providers typically yields more accurate consensus estimates.)

Estimize provides a specific rationale for its participants' ability to produce projections that are more accurate than the average sell-side estimates available on Yahoo! Finance and Bloomberg. Estimize claims that its estimate providers are incentivized to provide accurate forecasts. In contrast, sell-side analysts' forecasting accuracy might be biased by other incentives, including their objective of obtaining investment banking business and corporate access from subject companies.

Estimize also asserts that its community of estimate providers includes "a wide range of individuals with different backgrounds and viewpoints." In addition to providing estimates from professional investors and analysts, Estimize counts among its ranks of contributors many nonprofessionals, including students and private investors. These community characteristics conform to the cognitive diversity prerequisite for the "wisdom of crowds" to function properly.

Although Estimize has an inclusive approach to crowdsourcing data, not all contributor estimates carry the same weight on its website. New contributors are evaluated based on the accuracy of their first five company projections. These estimates are "scrubbed" by Estimize's algorithm. Approximately 2.5 percent of all estimates are rejected because they are considered "unreliable." Outlier estimates—those that deviate materially from the average forecast for a particular company—are assigned greater weight if their contributors have developed favorable track records.

One of Estimize's incentives for contributors to be accurate is the inclusion of a Rankings web page on its website (see Exhibit 14). This page features a list of the most accurate earnings forecasters for the overall universe of Estimize contributors, for ten broad industry sectors, and for many more narrowly defined industry groups. The sector rankings are based on individual participant accuracy scores, which range between –25 to +25 points, depending on the distance that a particular contributor's forecast is from a company's reported result.

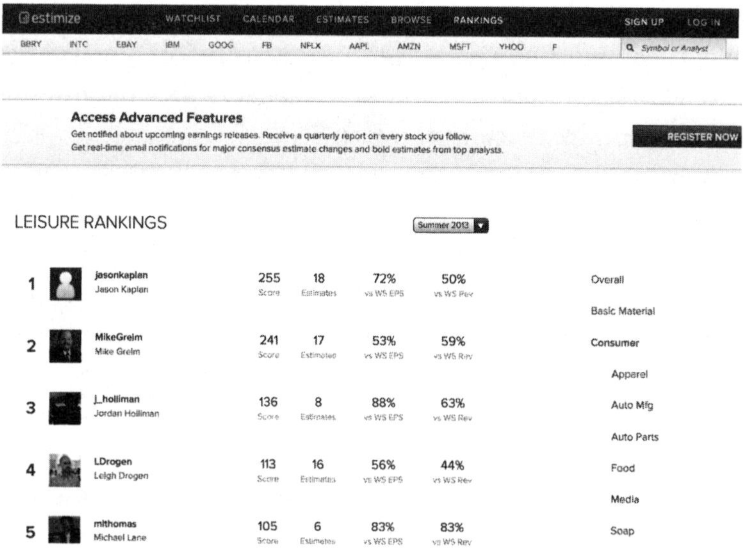

Exhibit 14: *www.Estimize.com* **"Rankings" Web Page for the Leisure Industry**
Source: *www.Estimize.com.*

Even though Estimize is not a social media website in the conventional sense, it retains many of the interactive aspects of other social media applications. The website encourages user reciprocity. Individuals benefit from access to consensus projections from the contributor community, but are also expected to contribute their own projections to the Estimize database.

I recently met with Leigh Drogen, Estimize's CEO, who explained how the website is different from other investment-related social media tools. In developing Estimize, Drogen's objective was to create a medium for financial data-sharing that is open and inclusive of many types of contributors, but is also structured and rigorous.

The Estimize platform can be integrated with your LinkedIn, Twitter, or StockTwits accounts. In order to bolster its institutional presence, Estimize signed a licensing agreement with Bloomberg. As a result, the ubiquitous Bloomberg data and news service terminals used by professional traders and investors feature Estimize's earnings forecasts.

One of the compelling features of Estimize is that it does not charge users a subscription fee. You can subscribe to estimate alerts and contribute your own forecasts without paying a dime. So how does Estimize make money? By selling its data to professional investors, such as hedge funds and traders, who pay fees to obtain access to Estimize's Application Programming Interface, or API. (An API is a technology feature that creates an interface between a data provider's software and a data user's software. The important role of APIs is discussed at greater length in Chapter 9.) According to Pando Daily (*www.pando. com*), a website that focuses on Silicon Valley, some hedge funds pay between $3,000 and $15,000 per month to obtain access to Estimize's data API.

Estimize and P/E

Estimize has a strong following among institutional investors, but is it a useful tool for individual investors? The answer really depends on how granular and analytical you are in conducting investment research. Many investors gauge whether a stock is undervalued or overvalued by calculating its price-to-earnings (P/E) ratio, which represents the market value of the company divided by its earnings. A stock with a lower P/E ratio is generally considered more attractively valued. A company's stock might trade at a higher P/E ratio if that company maintains a faster rate of earnings growth, or if it generates a higher rate of return on the investment of its capital.

In order to calculate P/E ratios, investors frequently rely on consensus earnings estimates supplied by Yahoo! or Bloomberg. For these investors, Estimize consensus data can be a powerful supplemental resource—and one that is free. By dividing the market price of a company's stock by its earnings-per-share estimate, supplied by Estimize, you can arrive at a P/E multiple that reflects the consensus expectations of an investor universe that is broader and more diverse than the sell-side analyst community. In view of Estimize's track record of predictive accuracy, the availability of an alternative P/E ratio, based on the "Estimize consensus," might prove to be a useful reference point for some investors. This is particularly true for investors in companies for which analysts have not been able to forecast financial results with a great degree of accuracy.

Drogen is exploring other ways to use Estimize's crowdsourcing technology in order to provide useful information for investors. In March 2014, Estimize announced that the company had launched an affiliate operation, called Mergerize. Drogen believes that Mergerize's focus on "crowdsourcing expectations for mergers and acquisitions" will offer investors new insights into a wide range of corporate actions, including spinoffs, equity offerings, and corporate buyouts. Mergerize might prove to be a useful online venue for corporate managers to assess investor expectations about potential acquisition targets and prices. Using Mergerize, quantitative and event-driven traders might also benefit by comparing their proprietary expectations about prospective business combinations with those of "the crowd."

In the future, Estimize might offer consensus data for financial estimates other than revenues and earnings. Drogen understands that his company is providing a powerful medium for compiling and analyzing its users' projections of stock valuation multiples and economic metrics. On April 23, 2014, Estimize announced that it would begin to track contributor estimates for seventeen U.S. economic indicators, including gross domestic product (GDP), payroll, housing, durable goods, and inflation data. In the future, the company intends to track additional economic data forecasts.

SumZero: A Crowdsourcing Tool for Professional Investors

SumZero (*www.sumzero.com*) was founded in 2008 by Divya Narendra, who had previously been the cofounder of ConnectU, an early competitor of Facebook. SumZero describes itself as a "reciprocity-based" investing and financial platform. Its members are required to share certain types of information in order to obtain access to research ideas provided by the website's network of approximately 10,000 members.

According to the company's website, individuals must apply for membership, and agree to submit at least one original research report every six months, in order to obtain access to SumZero's research reports and financial models databases. Having met this research-sharing requirement, SumZero members are not required to pay a fee for membership in the website's community of investors, whose professional background details are included in their online profiles.

Unlike Estimize, its neighbor in Manhattan's Silicon Alley, SumZero requires that its prospective members be affiliated with buy-side investment firms, including mutual funds, hedge funds, and private equity firms. This membership requirement stands in contrast to that of the more inclusive Estimize, which counts sell-side brokerage analysts, students, and other non-buy-side–affiliated individuals among its members.

SumZero is closely watched in the social media industry, in part because of the firm's affiliation with some well-known technology investors. Tyler and Cameron Winklevoss, famous for their lawsuit against, and subsequent legal settlement with, Facebook founder Mark Zuckerberg, were reported to have invested $1 million in SumZero. SumZero CEO Narendra, as well as Tyler and Cameron Winklevoss, are all alumni of Harvard University, where they had been classmates, and cofounders of the social networking website ConnectU.

SumZero also made a bit of a splash in hedge-fund industry circles when the company set up a database that enables investment professionals to compare anonymously their compensation levels with those of professionals in similar job roles at other investment firms. Like other features of SumZero, the compensation database is "reciprocity-based." Non-buy-side investors are invited to apply for a limited form of SumZero membership that entitles them to receive periodic news headlines, weekly e-mails featuring member investment recommendations, as well as access to buy-side job listings and member events.

SumZero's "Weekly Market Dispatches," a free product available to non-buy-side investor subscribers, include company research reports with financial projections, price targets, and valuation analyses. The weekly mailings contain calendars of upcoming earnings announcements, news about hedge funds, and portfolio manager profiles. Readers can also find the results of member surveys, some of which poll the website's contributors about their expectations for global stock market returns, industry developments, and securities market risks.

Other Curating Websites

There are other investment and financial websites that position themselves as curators of Internet-based content. StreetEYE (*www.streeteye.com*) is one such site. It incorporates a voting mechanism in order to generate a list of "today's top financial market news, as voted by you." StreetEYE sources its headlines from Twitter and financial blogs, and ranks items based on the frequency with which they are shared by other users of social media platforms.

Each StreetEYE headline item is assigned a "hotness" index. That index is based on the number of visitors who either share, up-vote, or click on the headline. As a result, StreetEYE, as a curator of online content, tends to feature social media contributors who are widely followed, socially influential, or actively engaged in sharing content with other members of the online community. Like many social finance websites, StreetEYE employs a social reciprocity system under which users are "rewarded" with higher rankings and more community credibility in exchange for being generous with their sharing of blog posts and news.

Users of StreetEYE can choose to follow "top news," "all news," "Twitter leaders," or "blog leaders." Many of the leading financial blogs discussed in Chapter 3 also appear on StreetEYE's list of leading blogs. The posts on these blogs are shared by, or linked to, the blogs of many other online visitors. Not surprisingly, StreetEYE's list of Twitter leaders includes the names of prominent bloggers and social website operators (discussed in other parts of this book).

It might appear to new users of curated investing websites like StockTwits and StreetEYE that a general consensus exists about the identity of the financial web's opinion leaders and top social connectors. StreetEYE's inclusion of a social voting mechanism, and its objective of featuring top financial news as determined by a voting process, bear similarities to the social bookmarking website applications that are discussed in Chapter 8.

LinkedIn Interest Groups

LinkedIn (*www.linkedin.com*) has become a vital resource for online professional networking and career advancement. Anyone wishing to develop her or his career skills and business networks should take advantage of its resources. Users can join professional interest groups that offer members opportunities for information-gathering, networking, and job-hunting. These groups are curated by group managers and feature the crowdsourcing characteristics that warrant their inclusion in a chapter about community-based social media.

Participating in a LinkedIn professional interest group requires that you submit a request for membership to the group's manager, who then approves your eligibility. You can join multiple groups, several of which are particularly relevant to stock market investors. Once you are approved to join a LinkedIn group, you can obtain access to that group's web page by selecting the "Groups" option in the "Interests" pull-down menu button, which is located on the top menu of the LinkedIn homepage. Prospective group members can obtain information about a group by reviewing its Profile, which includes a description of the group's mission. Each group also shares some of its statistics, which include the group's activity and growth, as well as composite data about existing members' job functions, industry affiliations, and locations.

The LinkedIn group summaries that follow are presented in descending order of the size of group membership. The standard features of a LinkedIn professional group include a membership database, sorted by the proximity of members to one's own professional network; a series of discussions about topics pertinent to group members; and a list of descriptions of industry-related jobs, posted by members who have approached the group for recruiting purposes. Although the discussion forums on LinkedIn group web pages contain valuable information, joining these groups is a worthwhile endeavor if only for the associated networking benefits.

Equity Research Analysts

The Equity Research Analysts group, with approximately 14,000 members, was launched in August 2008. The group targets experienced equity research professionals who have an interest in sharing information about stock research and professional opportunities. Group discussion topics have included sector-specific industry trends, stock research reports, and trends in commodities and currencies trading.

Emerging Market Investment Professionals Network

The Emerging Market Investment Professionals Network, with about 10,700 members, is for investors who have an interest in corporate finance, asset management, private equity, fund management, and trading. The emerging economies addressed in the group's discussion forums include Russia, India, China, Brazil, and Turkey. Another group of similar size, the Emerging Market Equity Investors Network, hosts discussions about political and economic issues confronted by professionals who are active in emerging markets.

Two More Groups

Two other investment-related LinkedIn groups are worthy of mention. The Value Investing Congress group, formed in 2009, was organized to support the interests of members involved in an annual conference bearing the same name. The conference is typically attended by institutional investors, who are self-described "value investors." Discussion topics on the group's LinkedIn page include behavioral finance, stock ideas, and commentary on conference-related events.

The Association of Technical Market Analysts group focuses on the "theory, practice, and application" of financial technical analysis, according to the group's description on LinkedIn.

Technical analysis involves the study of trading chart patterns and related statistical data in order to gauge the future direction of securities prices. Past discussion topics in this LinkedIn group have included stock, currency, and index trading ideas, as well as information about technical analysis conferences and professional certifications.

Ideas from the Crowd: Can You Trade on Them?

Beyond using these websites as information sources, is there a way to put the wisdom of crowds into action? For those individuals interested in entrusting their investing decisions to the opinion leaders who emerge on websites like StockTwits, new mechanisms are evolving that facilitate crowd-based trading.

In May 2013, StockTwits announced an agreement with a retail broker called Ditto Trade, a self-described "social investing firm." Ditto Trade's defining feature is that it offers customers the ability to participate in the actual trades of more experienced investors. By "attaching" oneself to a lead trader, such a customer can automate the trading process and "piggyback" on the stock trades of lead investors.

StockTwits members who are willing to provide trading and alert updates to Ditto Trade (*www.dittotrade.com*) can participate in the trading activity of other individuals they follow, as identified by their trader profiles on Ditto Trade. Those StockTwits participants who do not elect to trade alongside Ditto Trade's "lead traders" still have the option of receiving mobile alerts from some of these leaders.

It is unclear how many StockTwits members actually relinquish control over some of their investing decisions and "crowd trade" in this manner. I suspect that few individuals, even if they subscribe to the crowdsourcing analysis approach, would be willing to put their trading decisions on "autopilot" and trust crowdsourced opinion leaders, no matter how well the crowd's inputs are curated.

Whatever the degree of involvement in crowd trading by social media participants, the StockTwits–Ditto Trade solution is another indication that social investing is emerging as a credible alternative to the conventional practice of conducting research and buying or selling stocks as a solitary undertaking. Other recent innovations in the field of social trading are described in Chapter 10.

Key Takeaways from Chapter Five

- The ascension of crowdsourced social media websites for investors traces its origin to a behavioral finance concept known as the "wisdom of crowds."
- Investors can customize narrowly filtered "streams" on Stock-Twits to follow other investors' comments about specific stocks or investment topics.
- StockTwits's Social Heatmap enables users to monitor the frequency and volume of social media messages generated by the website's users.
- Websites such as Estimize produce financial projections that are more accurate than the average sell-side estimates available on websites operated by Yahoo! and Bloomberg.
- SumZero is a reciprocity-based online community that crowdsources financial models and reports from its members, who are required to be buy-side investors.

CHAPTER SIX

Financial Media Websites

The financial websites of leading Internet companies, such as Yahoo!, Google, and AOL, are not social media applications in the same sense as Twitter and Facebook. However, they provide an important data source and news portal for investors and incorporate several features that underscore the benefits of using social media to inform investment decisions. For example, Yahoo! Finance streams messages from third-party crowdsourcing investment websites, such as those discussed in Chapter 5, as well as blog articles from influential journalists.

In this chapter we'll look at several of the essential features of Yahoo! Finance that investors can use to track the performance of customized portfolios, review stock charts, and download stock price data. We will also look at how that website delivers access to company trading statistics, financial metrics, and data about industry competitors. From there we'll consider the limitations of, and risks associated with, financial website message boards, as well as the benefits of using Yahoo! Finance and Dow Jones's MarketWatch to track curated social media streams and financial blog posts. We'll then review several important searching tools available on Google Finance, as well as a series of investment and portfolio-tracking and information resources that can be found on AOL's DailyFinance website (*www.dailyfinance.com*).

Yahoo! Finance and Other Financial Data Portals

Despite their useful features, many investors underuse services provided by Yahoo! Finance, Google Finance, and DailyFinance. Financial analysts at many Wall Street firms have access to the paid services provided by leading financial news and data vendors such as Bloomberg and Thomson Reuters, and for this reason may not use free services such as these. But for professional analysts and investors who follow certain commodity-driven sectors, such as basic materials, energy, or agribusiness, paid subscription services such as Bloomberg may be a necessity. As well, some individual investors may not take advantage of these free services because they are able to obtain news feeds and access financial databases that are included with their online brokerage accounts. However, smaller research companies with limited budgets might not use fee-based subscription services. As a result, many financial professionals who operate on a smaller scale turn to free financial websites for investment news and data. Like these professionals, if you can't afford access to fee-based data resources, you can use Yahoo! Finance, Google Finance, Daily-Finance, and others like them to get most of the financial and investing data you need.

Many of the examples included in this chapter involve the use of Yahoo! Finance, a popular investing website that serves as a useful template for demonstrating a wide range of online financial tools that are currently available. (Similar analytical tools and features can be found on both Google Finance and DailyFinance.)

Tracking Portfolios

One of the important first steps you should take when working with Yahoo! Finance is to create a customized stock portfolio. It is very likely that there are individual stocks that you own in your portfolio, or which you would like to follow closely, for other reasons. I'll be using a variety of Internet stocks as examples. These properties include Yahoo!, Google, Facebook, and LinkedIn. You can think of this as a social media portfolio. This portfolio also includes the NASDAQ Composite Index (represented by the symbol "^IXIC" on Yahoo! Finance), which provides a good benchmark against which to compare the performance of technology and Internet stocks.

To set up such a portfolio, simply establish a Yahoo! Finance account. Then select the "My Portfolios" navigation menu on the top of your Yahoo! Finance homepage and click the "Create Portfolio" option from the My Portfolio pull-down menu. After entering the stock symbols of the four Internet and social media companies previously mentioned, select the NASDAQ Composite Index as a benchmark. You will probably be interested in obtaining real-time data on these companies. To do so, select the "Real-Time" default view option. In order to receive free real-time data from Yahoo! Finance, simply activate the "Streaming Quotes" option on your Yahoo! Finance homepage.

Yahoo! Finance will generate a default portfolio view for you. It will include each stock symbol you selected, the time and price of the most recent stock quote, and the dollar change and the percentage change in the stock since the close of the prior day's trading session. The Recent News headlines feature a reverse chronologically ordered stream of news stories that are associated with all of the stock symbols in your customized portfolio.

Even though the default portfolio view rendered by Yahoo! Finance provides a useful information snapshot, you might wish to customize your portfolio further by selecting "Add Custom View" on the top of your portfolio screen. You can then customize your portfolio to reflect specific metrics that you want to track. For the aforementioned social finance portfolio, consider including the following trading metrics:

- *Company name and symbol:* This field provides the basic identifying information for each stock in the portfolio.
- *Last trading price:* Yahoo! Finance provides a real-time data feed that includes quotes for NYSE and NASDAQ stocks, based on the NASDAQ "Last Sale."
- *Dollar and percentage change:* It's a good idea to track the absolute change, as well as the percentage change, of a stock's price since the prior day's close.
- *Current-day trading volume and average daily trading volume:* In order to gauge a stock's trading liquidity, it's useful to track how many shares have changed hands during the current trading session, relative to the stock's average trading volume.
- *Fifty-two-week trading range:* This metric allows you to keep track of whether a stock is trading near the top, bottom, or middle of its trading range over the past twelve months.
- *Market capitalization:* This field includes updated estimates of the market value of each company in your portfolio. Market value is the company's stock price, multiplied by its outstanding shares.

In addition to using these metrics, you can annotate your customized portfolio with comments or reminders about particular stocks.

Generating Historical Data

Another valuable feature of Yahoo! Finance is the ability of users to tap into the stock price database that drives its price charts. You can obtain access to this historical stock price data by selecting the "Historical Prices" option in the navigation menu. You can also generate a data series of stock prices (including open, high, low, and closing prices), as well as trading volumes, on a daily, weekly, or monthly basis. These data series, which are available over longer timeframes, can be downloaded into a spreadsheet to facilitate other types of analyses. Professional analysts use information from Yahoo! Finance's historical stock price database to calculate total return and percentage gain statistics for stocks over specified time periods.

Company Profiles, Competitors, and Statistics

Analysts often use Yahoo! Finance at the initial stages of company research, when they are trying to develop a basic familiarity with the company's fundamental and trading characteristics. They use this data to determine the company's suitability for additional research, or as a benchmark for comparable valuation analysis. Each company's profile page on Yahoo! Finance includes a summary of its business operations, a description of its investment sector affiliation, and a list of its senior management executives.

The "Competitors" page provides a list of companies engaged in similar lines of business, as well as a summary of those companies' market values and financial characteristics. On Yahoo! Finance, the list of comparable companies provided for LinkedIn includes other Internet companies, such as Facebook and Monster Worldwide.

Another useful feature of Yahoo! Finance's company summaries is the "Key Statistics" page, which renders a snapshot of valuation metrics, financial statement highlights, and trading statistics. Yahoo! Finance draws this data from multiple sources, including Thomson Reuters, EDGAR Online, and Morningstar, Inc. (*www.morningstar.com*). While you could get these data sets directly from these and other sources, having them consolidated in a single site will save you time and effort.

The "Key Statistics" page on Yahoo! Finance provides several important statistics with which every investor should be familiar:

- *Shares outstanding and float:* LinkedIn has approximately 121 million shares outstanding, but its "free float"—those shares freely available for purchase by investors, excluding shares held by corporate insiders—is 102 million shares. Many investors focus on a company's float as an indication of its liquidity, or the ease with which you could buy or sell its stock.

- *Percentage held by insiders and institutions:* According to Yahoo! Finance, about 1 percent of LinkedIn shares are owned by corporate insiders. Nearly 90 percent of the company's shares are held by institutional investors.

- *Total shares short as a percentage of float:* Investors sometimes borrow shares and then sell them short, based on the expectation of future price declines. A large short interest could indicate a high degree of pessimism about a company's future performance, but it could also set up the possibility of a "short squeeze." This could occur if a constructive event were to impel investors with a short interest in a stock to cover their short positions by purchasing shares of the stock that they had previously borrowed. In the case of LinkedIn, the 4.2 million shares held short represent a comparatively modest 4.6 percent of the company's float.

General Investing Features

Yahoo! Finance includes several useful features that provide additional context for understanding stock-specific developments. Stock investors frequently refer to the "Market Movers" table (on the "Finance Home" navigation menu page) of Yahoo! Finance to identify the market's largest stock price percentage gainers and losers during a particular trading session. The "Market Data—Stocks" navigation menu web page includes a summary of worldwide stock market indices. This feature enables investors to understand the performance of the U.S. equities market in the context of other global stock markets.

The "Market Data—Currencies" navigation menu page provides summaries of major currency exchange rates, as well as a selection of regional currency pairs. The "Currencies Center" also provides a useful currency conversion application that enables investors to convert monetary values from one currency to another. You can customize this feature to provide foreign exchange conversion estimates for previous trading sessions. If you focus on commodity-driven sectors, such as energy, metals, or agribusiness, Yahoo! Finance provides a useful compendium of commodities data. The "Market Data—Commodities Futures" navigation menu web page provides trading levels for short-term futures contracts for energy, metals, grains, and livestock commodities.

"Market Pulse" and Journalist Blogs

Yahoo! Finance has adapted several features that incorporate important social media elements, including financial blogs and crowdsourced investing websites, which are described in Chapters 3 and 5, respectively. In December 2010, Yahoo! Finance announced the launch of "Market Pulse," describing it as an "aggregated stream of information from around the Web." The "Market Pulse" feature includes a stream of messages from Stock-Twits and Covestor, another social finance website. In order to launch "Market Pulse," Yahoo! agreed to purchase StockTwits's Application Programming Interface (API). "Market Pulse" features a list of "Trending Tickers," which include the symbols of those stocks that are currently attracting the greatest volume of social media message activity. Yahoo! conceived of "Market Pulse," and its "Trending Tickers" data feed, as a tool for investors who, as they say, "find it cumbersome to navigate from one site to another on the Web."

"Market Pulse" visitors can engage other users by "Liking" their messages on Facebook, or by "tweeting" them on Twitter. This is a useful feature for investors who wish to peruse social media messages about stocks, while using the other resources offered by Yahoo! Finance. Investors who wish to contribute their own views and comments to StockTwits discussion strings might prefer instead to visit StockTwits directly, or to contribute to those discussions through their Twitter or Facebook accounts, which can also be integrated with StockTwits.

In recent years, Yahoo! Finance has boosted the prominence of its editorial content with the addition of well-known print and broadcast journalists. These financial columns and video posts can be found by way of the "Yahoo Originals" link on the homepage of Yahoo! Finance. In March 2011, Jeff Macke, a flamboyant former hedge fund manager and former panelist on CNBC's *Fast Money* show, joined Yahoo! Finance. Mr. Macke's video comments and written articles appear in a blog called *Breakout* (*www.finance.yahoo.com/blogs/breakout*). *Breakout* bills itself as Yahoo! Finance's "interactive investing show, offering fresh segments throughout the investing day." Macke and Josh Brown, CEO of Ritholtz Wealth Management, are co-authors of the book *Clash of the Financial Pundits*, which was published in April 2014.

Michael Santoli, a former associate editor and award-winning columnist at Dow Jones's financial periodical, *Barron's*, joined the Yahoo! Finance team in October 2012. Santoli is the author of another Yahoo! Finance blog, *Unexpected Returns*. A frequent guest commentator on CNBC, Santoli writes about financial market trends, and discusses geopolitical catalysts and high-profile stocks that are in the news.

Two other prominent financial journalists, Aaron Task and Henry Blodget, make regular appearances on *Daily Ticker*, a video series on Yahoo! Finance recorded against a television studio backdrop. Task is editor-at-large for *TheStreet*. Blodget, a former Internet sector equity research analyst and a hyperki-netic speaker, is the CEO and editor-in-chief of Business Insider, a widely followed source of financial news. The narrative content featured on Yahoo! Finance might take an even more "social" turn in the wake of the September 2013 hiring of Phil Pearlman as its interactive editor. Pearlman, a former hedge fund manager, was a cofounder and executive editor of StockTwits.

A Cautionary Note about Stock Message Boards

It is ironic that one of the more "social" resources offered by Yahoo! Finance, as well as by other general-audience financial websites, is a feature you should probably avoid: the message boards.

The quality of comments provided by message board users on Yahoo! Finance tends to be quite uneven. These message boards are often cluttered with off-topic (or off-color) comments, self-serving or disparaging remarks, and purely anecdotal observations masquerading as research viewpoints. These pages include long strings of inter-user bickering, as well as obscure inside jokes and references.

Leigh Drogen, the CEO of Estimize, provided a blunt characterization of the impact on social finance from the pseudonymous message posts found on financial website message boards, such as those operated by Yahoo! Finance. In a December 2013 blog article, he observed that "our social finance predecessors, specifically the Yahoo! Finance message boards, basically ruined pseudonymity for everyone by being a free-for-all garbage pile of pump and dump rumors." The legacy of these message boards has made it difficult for investors to "believe it was possible to get good info from someone without a real name attached." (Observing that "finance people have a really hard time signing up for a platform with a pseudonym," Drogen decided to permit users of Estimize to choose between using their real names or having a username assigned to them.)

Yahoo! Finance's message boards have been updated to include a "thumbs up, thumbs down" voting mechanism. Even with this attempt to incorporate user feedback about the usefulness of message posts, these discussion boards still suffer from many of the drawbacks characteristic of noncurated Internet comment pages and so-called chat rooms. If you want to learn more about the opinions and analyses of other traders, you're better off visiting StockTwits or some of the other professionally curated websites (see Chapter 5).

StockTwits's Message Streams

The StockTwits imprimatur and online curators provide no assurances about the quality of analysis and commentary appearing on that company's website. However, the discussion strings on StockTwits tend to be more serious-minded than those found on the message boards of major financial websites, such as Yahoo! Finance, which cater to a more general audience.

An Example of the Wide Reach of Yahoo! Finance

Yahoo! Finance is used by a broad audience of investors and stock market followers, some of whom are among the youngest members of the Millennial Generation. In May 2013, Yahoo! Finance reporter Lauren Lyster appeared at the 2013 Internet Week New York (IWNY) conference, where she moderated a panel on "Financial Education for the Next Generation via Online and Social Media." One of the panel participants interviewed by Lyster was a sixteen-year-old actress named Rachel Fox who had appeared on the television series *Desperate Housewives*.

Fox had recently taken on the improbable persona of a day trader, financial website publisher, and stock market blogger, with about 10,000 followers on Twitter. During her appearance at the IWNY Conference, Fox explained that she began trading equities after learning about the stock market from her parents. She observed, "I go on Yahoo! Finance every single morning. I look up all my stock information there." Fox also mentioned that she sometimes conducts cashtag-based stock searches on Twitter before executing securities trades.

Social media consultant, Stephanie Grayson, who was then social media editor for Yahoo! Finance, also spoke on the IWNY panel. She cited a survey, "The Future of Investing and the Great Social Shift," which was published by Marketwired (*www.Marketwired.com*) in May 2013. As noted by Grayson, the survey revealed that "60 percent of people who are under the age of forty . . . regularly consult social media for investment purposes."

Another Useful Snapshot of
Social Media Sentiment

MarketWatch (*www.marketwatch.com*) is a financial news and information website published by Dow Jones, a subsidiary of News Corporation. According to MarketWatch, its website and app attract more than 16 million monthly visitors. MarketWatch features data and news from several information providers, including CNBC, *Seeking Alpha*, and a financial information provider called Market IQ.

Market IQ analyzes unstructured data from social media websites, news outlets, and blogs. The social media data APIs ingested by Market IQ include those supplied by Twitter, Stock-Twits, LinkedIn, and Facebook. Market IQ analyzes these data, and then generates two data points known as Sentiment and Velocity. Market IQ's "Sentiment" indicator is based on the relative incidence of bullish and bearish sentiment for a stock. It is similar to the bullish and bearish sentiment indicators displayed on StockTwits. Market IQ's Velocity metric is described as an indicator of stock price volatility. It measures the current "buzz," or the volume of mentions of a security, across the unstructured data sources tracked by Market IQ.

The Market IQ Sentiment and "Velocity" charts visible to users of Dow Jones's MarketWatch website represent a high-level distillation of these data sets. They provide a general indication of social media sentiment but are not represented by Market IQ as actionable metrics. In other words, they are not financial measures on which investors might be expected to base an investment decision or action. The hedge funds that subscribe to Market IQ's "premium" app receive a more granular presentation of these data, including statistical analyses that underscore instances in which the Sentiment and Velocity indicators are most likely to predict future stock price returns.

Google Finance Domestic "Trends" Charts

Google's finance website offers similar features to those of Yahoo! Finance. Google Finance does, however, offer several unique resources. Clicking the "Google Domestic Trends" navigation menu option on Google Finance reveals a list of industry sectors and business and economic topics, such as bankruptcy, financial planning, and jobs. Select one of these categories and you'll call up a chart of search traffic for a business-related keyword, relative to the total search volume on Google.

For example, you could compare, for a specified time period, a time series of search activity for the term "travel" to the movements in stock indices or travel-related stocks. This travel index tracks Google search queries that are described by the Google Trends website as relating to "airlines, hotels, beaches, southwest, Las Vegas, [and] flights." The selected industry index is set to 1.0 as of 2004 and is displayed as a seven-day moving average. Alternatively, you can request a chart of search traffic for the term "Las Vegas" or a related query topic, such as "Vegas hotels," and use the results to compare either of those time series to a Google Trends chart for the broader sector category, "Travel."

For related business topic searches, you can turn directly to the Google Trends website (*www.google.com/trends*). On that website, you can compare search activity for terms, such as "Atlantic City" and "Las Vegas." These search results will include indications of regional interest, which represent the volume of searches under a topic, relative to the highest-level point of related searches on a world map. You could also review search metrics for related topics, such as "casino—accommodation type," or related queries, such as "casino Atlantic City."

Google Finance "Stock Screener" Feature

"Stock Screener" is another useful analytical feature unique to Google's finance website. It can be accessed from the main navigation menu of the Google Finance homepage. Using "Stock Screener," you can search for stocks that conform to particular financial criteria. These parameters include company market capitalization, P/E and other valuation ratios, dividend payout rates and yields, and profit margins. Investors can also specify other screening criteria, including revenue and profit growth rates, financial ratios that reflect corporate liquidity, balance sheet leverage, and operating rates of return.

As an investor, you can use Google "Stock Screener" to construct portfolios that meet certain investment requirements. For example, you could conduct a search for a list of all U.S. financial services entities with market capitalizations ranging between $500 million and $10 billion and that trade at a dividend yield of at least 1 percent. The resulting list of securities would likely include more than a dozen exchange-traded funds (ETFs) and bank and insurance holding companies.

AOL: DailyFinance

Another useful financial news and data portal is AOL's finance website, DailyFinance (*www.dailyfinance.com*). The AOL homepage includes four top-of-page navigation menu options that include "Plan," "Save," "Spend," and "Invest." Clicking on the Invest option brings up a number of Resources that include the "Daily Finance Investor Center" web page and the "Daily Finance Portfolios" web page.

The "Daily Finance Investor Center" features current-day trading gain and loss summaries for global equities, currencies, and futures markets, as well as a summary of the most active and largest-moving stocks on the New York Stock Exchange and the NASDAQ. Entering a stock symbol in the "Get Quote" search box on DailyFinance renders stock trading data, as well as a navigation menu that allows you to track sell-side analyst ratings, corporate insider trading activity, company growth rate statistics, financial ratios, and industry competitors. Users of the website can also obtain access to SEC financial documents, historical stock price and dividend data, as well as stock charts for individual companies. You can customize these stock charts to reflect different timeframes, frequencies, market index benchmarks, and comparable securities. These charting features resemble those found on Yahoo! Finance.

In addition, "Daily Finance Portfolios" allows users to set up a personalized stock portfolio, and then track the portfolio's performance, as well as monitor its gains and losses, trading charts, risk levels, and geographic exposures. You could also use the website's charting capabilities to compare the performance of one or more portfolios to that of market index benchmarks. Finally, using the News and Movers option on "Daily Finance Portfolios" allows you to monitor news headlines related to the stocks in your portfolio, and to track percentage movements of its individual security components. Many of these features resemble those available on Yahoo! Finance.

Key Takeaways from Chapter Six

- Yahoo! Finance provides useful and basic features for investors so that they can create and track portfolios and stock charts, and tap into historical stock price databases.

- Yahoo! Finance's "Market Data" and "Currencies Center" allow you to track market-wide movements in equity securities and currencies.
- Yahoo! Finance's "Market Pulse" provides you with access to a stream of messages from StockTwits and other social finance messaging services.
- While Yahoo! Finance features blog posts from noted journalists such as Michael Santoli and Henry Blodget, you should avoid its gossipy message boards.
- Google Finance's "Domestic Trends" and "Stock Screener" tools provide data visualization resources for measuring the volume of Internet search activity related to business keywords, as well as useful trading and financial screening utilities.

CHAPTER SEVEN

Stock Talk on Audio-Visual Platforms

Audio-visual media represent a powerful delivery platform for company and stock analysis. Many investors find video to be particularly useful for discerning trading patterns in stock charts. And the combination of audio narrative and visual presentations in an on-demand format can be a powerful medium for highlighting trading patterns and explaining investment recommendations. Because more investment advisors and publicly traded corporations rely on audio and video content to communicate with their clients and shareholders than ever before, it is important for you to be aware of the information that can be found on these podcasts and video recordings.

In this chapter, we'll talk about several examples of stock discussions and investing tutorials that can be found on YouTube, the video-sharing website owned by Google. You'll also learn how journalists, investment professionals, and finance scholars use the podcasting format to share insights with listeners; and how corporations, brokers, and consultants regularly use live webcasts to facilitate investor presentations. While audio and video deliveries are usually one-sided in nature, Google has introduced an interactive feature called "Hangouts," which facilitates live conversations that integrate photos and videos. We'll discuss this service in more detail later in this chapter.

YouTube Stock Discussions and Tutorials

An increasing number of investment professionals and stock market participants use YouTube (*www.youtube.com*) as a medium for explaining their views about stock ideas and for marketing financial advisory services. The informational resources on YouTube are by no means limited to the realm of stock investing. Individuals often turn to it for tutorials on a variety of subjects, ranging from home repair projects to consumer technology instruction.

As an individual investor, there are two reasons you're likely to visit YouTube. First, if you're seeking additional financial information—such as discussions about stock options or technical strategy—you may find YouTube to be a valuable resource. You can find videos featuring analyses of individual stocks by conducting cashtag-based searches on YouTube, much as you'd do on Twitter or StockTwits. Second, you can find useful videos that feature instructional presentations, including primers on technical analysis and equity valuation. Some of these videos are prepared by university lecturers and academics, while others are produced by securities industry practitioners.

Because YouTube is owned by Google, the video broadcasting platform uses the same search algorithms as other Google websites. Video broadcasters who are widely followed, and who make optimal use of subject "tags" that categorize their videos, are more likely to be featured prominently in YouTube search results.

A search on YouTube for the cashtag "$JCP" would reveal several videos that were recorded by a retailing analyst at Hedgeye (*www.hedgeye.com*), a research and financial media company that produces sector-based analysis (much of it prepared by analysts who had gained their experience at brokerage firm research departments). Hedgeye incorporates charts and data slides in its analysts' videos. Hedgeye, which also uses Twitter to publicize its investment ideas, generally produces videos of high production quality.

Another example of Hedgeye's prolific use of YouTube is its daily "Macro Notebook," which includes summaries of daily trends and trading activity. This broadcast is generally recorded either by Hedgeye's CEO or its director of research.

There are many examples of YouTube videos that offer instruction to investors. The quality and value of these videos vary, as does the knowledge base and the presentation skills of their preparers. By searching on YouTube under targeted terms, such as "technical analysis" or "stock valuation," you can obtain access to many of these videos. One prolific YouTube instructor is Tim Bennett, deputy editor of the UK-based financial periodical *MoneyWeek*. Bennett's presentations, while basic in their approach, are informative and easy to follow. Some of Bennett's more advanced tutorials include "What Is Technical Analysis?" and "What Is a Swap?"; and some of his more basic primers are "What Does Earnings per Share Mean?"; "What Is an Index?"; and "What Is a Stock Exchange?" If you're new to investing, these videos might be a good starting point for you.

The Twitter IPO

Investors should not rely exclusively on any one source of financial or valuation analysis. However, if you're trying to obtain insights into how stock professionals assess company valuations and analyze business models, instructional videos might be helpful to you. For example, in the days preceding, and immediately following, the November 2013 initial stock offering of Twitter, analysts and research managers at Hedgeye produced several YouTube videos that provided useful content for investors who wanted to become better acquainted with prevailing sentiment about the stock and to learn more about Twitter's business model.

Hedgeye, which took a decidedly bearish stance on the stock after its initial post-IPO run-up in price, produced video segments that offered several advantages over other media content offerings. The videos were beneficial to individual investors for several reasons:

- The videos were succinct and to the point, ranging in duration from three to six minutes.
- The speakers were effective at combining oral presentations with visual aids, including slides that presented summary points, company operating data, and valuation metrics.
- The presenters explained the basic elements of Twitter's business model in a manner that would have been clear even to those unfamiliar with the company's operations.
- Hedgeye made an unequivocal case for its bearish investment stance, which had been predicated on concerns about the sustainability of Twitter's revenue growth, as well as the stock's premium price-to-sales valuation multiple.

I am not endorsing the investment opinions expressed in Hedgeye's videos. Moreover, you should never make an investment decision based on the smattering of analytical content available in a single video. However, anyone who watched these broadcasts would have become much better informed about Twitter even if they had already reviewed the SEC financial documents, watched webcasts of management's investor presentations, and followed the press coverage of the company's stock offering plans.

Podcasting Presentations

The podcasting format might not strike you as the cutting edge of social media. Some of you might be aware that Twitter, one of the key players in today's social media revolution, emerged from the wreckage of Odeo, a podcasting start-up that had never gained traction and was ultimately rendered obsolete by Apple's iPod.

One of the best-known podcast-playing platforms is Apple's Podcasts app. Owners of iPads can download the app from their tablet's App Store. Useful podcasts can be found via Internet-based searches, or by searching on Apple's iTunes Store (*www.apple.com/itunes*). The advantage of listening to one of these audio-only downloads is similar to the benefit of listening to a conventional radio broadcast: Individuals can listen to segments while doing other work-related tasks. Think of them as the equivalent of free, on-demand business radio programs. While having an app like Apple's iTunes helps you maintain an updated feed of episodes from each podcast series, most podcast broadcasters provide direct access to their recordings on their blogs and websites.

A simple keyword-based search on the iPad's iTunes Store or Podcasts app under the term "technical analysis" calls up a list of technical analysis podcasts. Alternatively, Podcasts app users can search for news about a company, such as Apple itself, denoted by their stock symbol (AAPL). Such searches reveal a number of subscription-based services, such as Dan Fitzpatrick's "Chart of the Day" series and Bernie Schaeffer's "Options Update Podcast from Schaeffer's Investment Research." Those podcasts, which can be downloaded as MP4 files, include both audio-only and audio-visual content. Subscribing to one of these podcasting services enables you to be alerted when new broadcasts become available.

Several financial writers have compiled their own lists of well-known journalists who broadcast their views on regular podcasting shows. Among the financial podcasting series cited for their popularity are:

- *MarketWatch*, published by Dow Jones & Company
- Bloomberg's *Taking Stock*, hosted by Pimm Fox
- Morningstar's *Investing Insights*
- Consuelo Mack's *WealthTrack*

Bloomberg Radio features journalists whose programs can be accessed in podcast format via Bloomberg's free tablet or iPhone app. Bloomberg has an advantage in the podcasting realm because financial media followers are already familiar with its television and radio affiliates.

Pimm Fox, well known for his Bloomberg Television and Bloomberg Radio shows—as well as for his "made for radio" speaking voice—along with his cohost, Carol Massar, record podcasts of interviews and discussions about business and financial topics. Another well-known Bloomberg personality, Tom Keene, recognizable for his owlish appearance, raspy voice, and trademark bowtie, hosts a radio show called *Bloomberg Surveillance* that is available in podcasting format. His segment features author and business expert interviews.

Morningstar's *Investing Insights* program presents, in magazine-style interview format, multiple viewpoints on investment and economic topics, such as the Federal Reserve's decision to taper its bond-buying program, U.S. federal budget deliberations, and "Black Friday" holiday season retail sales. Like Bloomberg's on-demand podcasts, these recordings have the sound and feel of business news radio shows.

Michael Covel is a financial author and speaker. He has produced more than 250 episodes of a podcast series called *Trend*

Following. Covel claims that his podcast series has been listened to more than 2 million times by followers in 182 countries and territories. Trend following refers to a series of commodities and equities trading strategies that identify entry and exit points based on proprietary systems. Like other forms of technical analysis, trend following represents a departure from the "buy and hold" strategy used by many stock investors. Covel interviews prominent traders who discuss their investing styles and the financial implications of public policy decisions. Investors are likely to find the podcast series informative and engaging, regardless of whether they base their investment decisions on company fundamentals and valuation metrics, or on technical analysis.

Mark Fane, a California-based certified retirement counselor, is a self-described big fan of Covel's books and podcasts. He applies trend-following strategies to small-capitalization stock trading. Fane describes the *Trend Following* podcast as a "meta-valuable" source of insight into the systems employed by professional traders. Interviews with these traders are aggregated on Covel's website. Podcast listeners such as Fane have the opportunity to learn how prominent traders handle wins and losses. Covel's interview with Ed Seykota, a commodities trader who speaks extensively about trend following, has been cited by Fane as a particularly memorable podcast.

Jan Urbahn, an operations executive with an automotive engineering background, also closely follows Michael Covel's investing podcasts. Urbahn cites as particularly memorable an October 2013 interview with Larry Williams, a financial author and stock and commodities futures trader. Urbahn observes that he learned a great deal from Williams's description of how he trades "with very little risk" by containing the size of his investments. This approach appears to enable Williams to bear multiple investment losses in a credible fashion. In the interview, Covel asked

Williams about the lessons he has learned during his investment career.

The availability of podcasting apps, like Apple's Podcasts, has enabled finance students and practitioners to access the lectures of influential business scholars. Aswath Damodaran, a professor of finance at the Stern School of Business at New York University, has been conducting online finance courses since 1998. Damodaran was ranked by CNNMoney as one of the top-ten business school professors in the world. His presentations on the subject of corporate valuation are available on YouTube and on Apple's iTunes U app. (Some educators use these apps to record lectures.)

In 2013, Professor Damodaran produced a free online valuation course, which consists of 137 recordings. One of his podcast lectures, an eighteen-minute-long segment entitled "The Basics of Relative Valuation," demonstrates Damodaran's ability to engage his listeners. The recording describes the merits and mechanics of intrinsic and relative stock valuation methodologies. Damodaran is adept at blending academic explanations with practical observations about the types of valuation techniques employed by securities industry professionals. His recorded lectures and slides blend analytical rigor with a down-to-earth, easy-to-follow presentation style.

Other Internet-Based Sources of Video Content on Investing

In recent decades, investors have benefited from two parallel regulatory and technological developments. These developments have significantly affected how public corporations communicate with their stakeholders. First, in 2000, the SEC adopted Regulation FD, which addressed the long-standing issue of the selective disclosure by companies of material nonpublic information. The rule requires companies with material news to file a Form 8-K, or to use other acceptable methods of broad dissemination, including conference calls and Internet-based transmissions. Second, two popular software programs introduced during the 1990s, RealNetworks's RealPlayer and Microsoft's Windows Media Player, allow anyone with an Internet connection to obtain real-time access to webcasts of company financial presentations, or to replay those webcasts.

Regardless of your approach to investment decision-making, you should take advantage of the audio-visual content and slide presentations available on company investor relations websites. One of the first steps many financial analysts take when trying to learn about a company is to replay the last several available earnings conference calls, or to review the printed transcripts of those calls. These recordings not only recap important business developments but also provide an opportunity to assess how effectively corporate executives respond to questions from institutional investors. Issues of over-arching importance are likely to be addressed during question-and-answer sessions over the course of several quarters. You can stay abreast of business trends by listening to these conference call webcasts. However, listening to new webcasts without having first reviewed older call transcripts or recordings is akin to joining the middle of a fairly arcane conversation without any preparation.

Many companies make audio-visual broadcasts available on their investor relations websites, which they also use to host quarterly conference calls to discuss financial results. Investor relations managers provide access to similar presentations when companies host annual shareholder meetings, appear at brokerage firm–sponsored investor conferences, or host informational gatherings for institutional investors. Securities analysts can learn a great deal about companies by attending day-long analyst meetings or by participating in such meetings via webcast. These so-called Analyst Days generally feature presentations by company financial executives and by marketing and operational managers, who discuss different aspects of their business. The webcasting of such presentations offers individual investors the opportunity to have the same access to the informational slides, verbal overviews, and press releases as would any hedge fund manager. Google has taken the additional step of archiving its company's management presentations to investors on YouTube—a logical step because Google is the corporate owner of that website.

According to Quantcast, the CNBC website (*www.cnbc.com*) recently attracted approximately 12.9 million monthly unique visitors, well above the 10.3 million monthly unique visitors who had trafficked the website just three years earlier. Growth in the website's visitor traffic represents a marked contrast to the weak media trends exhibited by CNBC's cable network operation, which recently fell to a twenty-year low in ratings among the 25–54 age group.

CNBC.com disaggregates the cable network's uninterrupted flow of content, including video broadcasts on the CNBC cable network, into short segments. For investors with specific viewing interests, CNBC.com offers a menu of video options that include CEO interviews, analyst interviews, and clips of recent segments from the CNBC cable network. Just as the rollout of the iPod enabled music lovers to consume album tracks in the form of single-song MP3 files, rather than having to sit through an entire album, so CNBC has facilitated on-demand access to business news segments.

On Wall Street trading floors, wall-mounted televisions broadcasting CNBC are ubiquitous. However, since traders have neither the time (nor the inclination) to stay glued to their television screens, they often turn to social media for alternative ways to stay abreast of developments in the business world and financial markets. For example, you can follow the @CNBC Twitter feed for items of interest, and then turn to the CNBC website to see if a related video segment is available.

On December 27, 2013, about an hour and a half before the New York Stock Exchange's regular trading session began, a tweet appeared on the @CNBC Twitter feed that indicated an analyst at Macquarie Securities had downgraded his rating on Twitter's stock. In the wake of that news, the stock of Twitter declined 13 percent during that day's trading session. If you'd owned Twitter shares or had wished to follow market developments related to that stock, you could have visited CNBC's website to review media coverage about the rating change. Further, if you had visited CNBC.com and entered Twitter's stock symbol, TWTR, in the search box, you would have found, among other things, a three-minute-long video clip of a CNBC contributor posted at 10:30 A.M. that morning. The speakers appearing on this video clip discussed Twitter's stock price gains, valuation, as well as the dynamics that had driven investor interest in the social media sector. That video clip was accompanied by a written transcript of the on-screen interview.

Brokerage and Consulting Firm Audio-Visual Resources

If your objective is to obtain perspective on the outlook for the stock market or to learn more about specific trading and analytical techniques, many free resources are at your disposal. If you have an account with an online discount broker, such as Fidelity Investments, you might already have access to some of these services.

Fidelity's website includes a category called "News and Insights" that contains the web page called "Viewpoints." Recent Fidelity "Viewpoints" offerings include a series of videos and podcasts called "2014 Market Outlook," and "December

Market Update." Fidelity "Viewpoints" also features a series of topical articles under subject headings, like "Personal Finance" and "Investing Ideas."

If you're interested in exchange-traded funds (ETFs), and want to learn more about these products, another good online resource with helpful webinars would be the online publication ETF.com (*www.etf.com*). ETF.com markets several subscription-based data analytics services and sponsors a series of annual conferences about indexing and ETFs. If you are a newcomer to ETF.com, you would do well to access their webinars on basic trading and analytical techniques. Examples of free webinar subjects include "How to Trade ETFs," "Fixed Income ETFs," and "Index Methodology." ETF.com makes these webinars available with the expectation that some users will subscribe to its paid services. Nonetheless, you can get a lot of useful background information by viewing free webinars found there.

Google "Hangouts" and Related Google+ Services

Google has established a powerful presence across the social web. Writers can create personalized blogs using Google's content management system. Businesses can produce videos on Google's YouTube. Google+ (*www.plus.google.com*) has even tried to establish itself as a social networking community to compete with the "Likes" of Facebook. And the Google "+1" widget has become a popular way for readers to express their preference for blog posts and articles.

Because Google users interact with the company's various web-based services via a unified account, they are likely to encounter several features offered by the online search giant. One of these is Google "Hangouts" (*www.google.com/hangouts*), which Google launched in 2013. The product, which has been integrated with YouTube, offers video broadcasting capabilities. The service was developed to facilitate live, one-on-one conversations among Google account owners.

Whereas "Hangouts" is used for private video conferencing, a related service called "Hangouts On-Air" enables users to schedule and conduct live audio-visual broadcasts for audiences on both Google+ and YouTube. Recorded versions of these conversations are archived on YouTube. Google users can browse "Hangouts" that are currently on-air or look for future scheduled "Hangouts." Most "Hangouts" sessions have little to do with business or investing. However, stock market participants and business users are likely to make more extensive use of these services in the future.

While they fall outside the subject area of audio-visual services, several related Google features, also available through the Google+ interface, can serve as valuable investment research tools. One of the options available on Google+ is "Communities," which represents special interest groups that are akin to LinkedIn's professional interest groups and Facebook's interest groups. Google launched "Communities" in late 2012. Stock-related Google "Communities" include "Value Investing," and "Stocks and Investing Group." The "Value Investing Community" on Google+ features article links, blog posts, and stock research reports. The "Stocks and Investing Group," for its part, includes links to blog articles, stock charts, conference calls, and books related to the subject of investing.

Key Takeaways from Chapter Seven

- YouTube, owned by Google, can be a valuable source of video recordings of stock analyses and instructional presentations by market practitioners.

- Helpful instructional recordings are also available in podcast format on Apple's Podcasts app, on Bloomberg.com, or on various podcasters' websites.
- Corporate investor relations departments provide access to webcasts of earnings conference calls and analyst meetings on their company websites.
- Many investors have access to free informational videos and market outlook summaries via their online brokerage accounts.
- Investors can refer to CNBC.com for timely outtakes from the CNBC cable network.

CHAPTER EIGHT

Social Bookmarking Websites

Social bookmarking websites emerged in the last decade as a way for Internet users to store and organize their web page bookmarks online, rather than on their Internet browsers. In this chapter, we'll talk about the features of several of the more popular social bookmarking websites, including reddit, Delicious, Digg, StumbleUpon, and Pinterest. Among the websites profiled in this chapter, you'll probably find that reddit (*www.reddit.com*) contains the most useful source of stock-related commentary. The array of choices available among bookmarking websites might be a bit overwhelming; rather than plunge into them, you may hope it's sufficient to rely on the social media and crowdsourcing websites discussed in previous chapters. However, bookmarking apps can be great supplemental resources if you want to gain additional perspective on stocks.

The Role and Functions of
Social Bookmarking Websites

Social bookmarking websites are structured as online communities, accessible only to their members and subscribers. These websites rely on user community voting mechanisms to drive web page placement and rankings. Social bookmarking websites such as reddit and Digg (*www.Digg.com*) are sought after by avid Internet users who wish to communicate their likes and dislikes about the content they encounter online. However, since there are no universally accepted criteria that determine which linked articles should be upvoted or downvoted by users, it is often unclear whether highly ranked articles attain their stature by virtue of their relevance and timeliness or by their fit with often-subjective community criteria. The resulting page rankings on websites such as reddit are examples of online democracy at its best—and its worst.

In recent years, new bookmarking and content-sharing websites have emerged that serve a variety of specialized functions. The outcome of this proliferation has been a colorful patchwork of choices, represented by a series of quirky icons. Individuals can now use Vimeo for video sharing, Flickr or ShutterFly for photo sharing, and Newsvine for news article sharing.

Because many Internet users have come to rely on mainstream social media websites such as Facebook (*www.facebook.com*) and Twitter (*www.twitter.com*) for sharing links to documents, photographs, and videos, the future of social bookmarking is less clear than it might have appeared several years ago. Even so, Internet users are likely to continue to use social bookmarking venues because they have a lot of online content to share and organize, or because they embrace the convenience of saving favored webpage links to the "cloud" where they can be accessed from multiple desktop and mobile computing devices rather than from the web browser of a particular computer.

Social bookmarking websites offer a solution to the challenge of managing and indexing large volumes of online content. Some bookmarking venues have become useful destinations for finding background information about, or additional insights into, business research topics. However, stock market participants are likely to encounter a greater volume of relevant investment-related discussions on micro-blogging and crowdsourcing applications such as Twitter and StockTwits than on social bookmarking websites.

Profiles of Leading Social Bookmarking Websites

It should be stressed that the number of social bookmarking sites continues to grow, and they ebb and flow in popularity. Following is a review of some of the most popular at the time of this writing.

reddit (*www.reddit.com*)

According to Quantcast, reddit recently attracted 27 million monthly unique visitors. The site has emerged in recent years as a powerful force among operators of social media websites. The reddit website, which markets itself as "the front page of the Internet," has gained influence in determining the placement of content on the Internet. According to the *New York Times*, the reddit operation was spun off in 2011 from Advance Publications, a private media company, and has since functioned as an "operationally independent subsidiary" of that entity.

While using reddit is relatively straightforward, the website has several idiosyncrasies that might seem confusing to first-time visitors. Unlike most other websites, reddit is "community-curated," meaning that the placement of content on a page is determined by the net number of upvotes and downvotes from other reddit users. Within the reddit community these users are referred to as "redditors." According to reddit, the net vote total for a post that appears on the website is adjusted to eliminate the effects of spam. The placement of posts on reddit is also determined by a "time decay algorithm." Posted links and articles tend to move down in page ranking after a period of time, even if they had initially proven popular among readers.

Reddit places a premium on visitor contributions to group discussions. Website visitors can gain clout in the reddit community by posting helpful comments in response to other redditors' posts and questions. Acknowledgment of such community contributions is accorded by the awarding of "comment karma" points, which is a status symbol among reddit users.

Over time, redditors become familiar with the key tenets of "reddiquette," which the site describes as "an informal expression of [its] values." The values embraced by redditors include the importance of linking to original-source content and the avoidance of "blog spam," that is, the excessive posting of links to one's own website. Bloggers who inundate reddit with a large number of links to articles from their personal blogs might see those articles deleted by the website's spam filter.

In order to parse the wide range of topics discussed on the Internet, reddit has evolved into a series of topic-specific online communities, also known as "subreddits." These are essentially niche communities, where visitors can congregate to post comments, questions, and website links, or read posts by other redditors with similar interests.

Although reddit might appeal to a comparatively narrow niche of the online population, a surprisingly large percentage of redditors rely on the bookmarking website for their news consumption. According to Pew Research Center, while only 3 percent of the U.S. adult population uses reddit, a predominant 62 percent of reddit users turn to the website for news stories. In contrast, Facebook penetrates 64 percent of the adult population, making it the most popular social networking application on the web. However, less than half of its members use that website as a source of news.

There are several subreddits that might be of particular interest to stock investors. The "Security Analysis" subreddit (*www.reddit.com/r/SecurityAnalysis*) is devoted to the subject of value investing. This subreddit features a series of stock-specific posts, topical discussions (such as activist investing and corporate governance), as well as links to company financial documents.

The "Stock Market" subreddit (*www.reddit.com/r/StockMarket*) concentrates on "short and mid-term trading ideas, analysis, and commentary for active investors," according to that subreddit's member guidelines. Among the frequently cited topics on this subreddit are "equities, options, forex [foreign exchange market], futures, analyst upgrades and downgrades, technical analysis, and fundamentals."

The moderators of the "Stock Market" subreddit—the individuals who oversee this niche community on behalf of other redditors—encourage users to contribute posts about moving stocks, as well as observations about companies in the news. Topics discussed on this subreddit include analyst upgrades and downgrades of stocks, key macroeconomic news announcements, market sentiment indicators, and interpretations of the forces behind material moves in securities prices.

A third subreddit likely to be of interest to reddit visitors who are active in the stock market is the "Investing" community (*www.reddit.com/r/investing*). The moderators of the "Investing" subreddit encourage discussions about "news items relevant to investors," as well as the sharing of "investment ideas and insights," according to that subreddit web page. The message threads on this subreddit tend to be less stock-specific and more topical and question driven.

The "Investing" subreddit is geared toward investors who are trying to learn about specific financial subjects. Visitors to this subreddit include both professional and individual investors who are seeking to gain insight from its candid, open-ended discussions. For example, one buy-side equity analyst, despite having many other financial resources at her disposal, turned to the "Investing" subreddit for "suggestions for books or market news commentary," as well as for information about "what helps [other redditors] find stocks" and "get their ideas." According to this redditor, "that is something you can't really get from a finance textbook." This analyst also observed that the comment strings on reddit include some "great back-and-forth discussions about the style of investing." She believed that "the anonymity of people really makes this experience unique . . . because commenters and users are technically all equal and judged by the substance of their comments, as opposed to names and reputations." (The redditor quoted here preferred to maintain her anonymity.) While this "Investing" redditor acknowledged that the quality of reddit comments varies widely, she asserted that "the value of what [she] learned has far outweighed" the distractions associated with less valuable content on the website.

Delicious (www.delicious.com)

A recent article in a technology industry periodical chronicled the tenth anniversary of Delicious, a social bookmarking website that gained attention when Yahoo! acquired the company in 2005. Yahoo! sold Delicious to AVOS Systems in 2011. In May 2014, Science Media Inc. acquired Delicious from AVOS Systems. While Delicious offers a much cleaner-looking user interface than the heavily trafficked reddit, some observers believe that Delicious has lost its "cool factor" since its heyday in the mid-2000s decade.

According to Quantcast, the website traffic for Delicious recently stood at only 63,000 monthly unique visitors.

You can initiate searches for new information on Delicious by searching for items that have been "tagged" by other users as being relevant to a particular subject. This is done by using the hashtag "#[tagname]" convention familiar to Twitter users. Visitors to Delicious can alternatively search for another user's posts by typing "@[username]" in the search box. You can also search for tagged items for a particular topic or specific user by using the identifiers "@[username] #[tagname]." If you want to share your own content with other users, simply select Add Link, and then type the appropriate URL.

Digg (www.digg.com)

In 2004, technology entrepreneur Kevin Rose founded Digg. Rose developed the website as a way for him to organize and keep track of online news articles. Like Delicious, Digg is a social bookmarking website that has lost some luster in recent years. In 2012, Betaworks, a venture capital company, acquired Digg and redesigned the website. According to Quantcast, Digg recently attracted about 450,000 monthly visitors.

Searching for topics on Digg is relatively straightforward. After reviewing the online content rendered by a search, you can express your approval of selections by "digging" them (using the "Thumbs Up" icon, familiar to Facebook members). Alternatively, you can share items via your Facebook or Twitter accounts.

StumbleUpon (www.stumbleupon.com)

StumbleUpon is one of the oldest, and most heavily trafficked, social bookmarking websites. Founded in 2001, San Francisco–based StumbleUpon recently attracted 20.4 million monthly unique visitors, according to Quantcast. The website operation was acquired by eBay in 2007 but was subsequently spun off into an independent entity in 2009.

StumbleUpon users can choose from among a list of areas of interest, or search under specific subject areas, using the website's "Explore" feature, which directs its search engine to show relevant articles. StumbleUpon then hones in on the interests of its registered users by asking them to like or dislike the pages shown to them. Repeating these "Thumbs Up" and "Thumbs Down" selections enables the StumbleUpon search engine to select articles that conform to each user's narrowly defined areas of interest. You can also opt to follow other StumbleUpon members.

Pinterest (www.pinterest.com)

Pinterest, which is based in San Francisco, was founded in 2009. Pinterest is known for its flashy, bulletin-board-like user interface. Many Internet users associate the website with the posting of photographs of desserts, recipes, or wedding plan details, rather than with conducting investment-related research. However, the website, with its 59.2 million monthly unique visitors, as recently measured by Quantcast, has become an important player in the world of business-oriented social bookmarking.

Searching under a keyword or topic on Pinterest calls up a series of rectangular Post-it note–like boxes, which contain items that have been "pinned" by other Pinterest members who had found them interesting. Pinterest's bulletin board–like appearance, with its pinned articles, resembles the user interface of RSS reader Newsify (described in Chapter 4). A search for "Pins" under the term "value investing" yields an array of books, videos, infographics, and articles related to that subject. Alternatively, you can search for the "Boards," or collections of

Pins, that have been created by other Pinterest members with an interest in a particular topic.

> **A Word about Facebook**
>
> Facebook operates several social networking applications, including the Paper news-reading app (described in Chapter 4). The Facebook website is not typically categorized as a social bookmarking site. However, it can be very valuable as a business research tool. Many companies use their Facebook business pages to disseminate information about (and to promote) business projects, products, and corporate milestones. Company-sponsored Facebook pages can be a useful source of background information about a variety of corporate topics. Searching under relevant keywords using the Facebook search field gives you access to helpful articles, photographs, videos, and other online content.

Supplementing Investment Research

Conducting keyword-driven searches on social bookmarking websites can be an effective way to supplement your company and industry research. Bookmarking websites often prove useful in identifying additional background information that you might not find elsewhere. I recently used several bookmarking websites to obtain additional insights into consumer perceptions about MGM Resorts International's resort development plans in Springfield, Massachusetts, where MGM was recently awarded a gaming license. I also used bookmarking apps to find information about a planned gaming project at Maryland's National Harbor, where MGM Resorts was also recently awarded a casino license.

The Facebook business page for MGM Springfield featured a collection of newspaper articles, promotional videos, career workshop updates, chamber of commerce meeting announcements, corporate press releases, and newsletters related to the proposed casino plan. These company-sponsored information sources tended to emphasize the project's potential community benefits and general business attributes, rather than its financial characteristics.

Further, I used reddit to find candid discussion strings about business topics relevant to this particular project. In one online exchange about the MGM casino proposal, a Las Vegas–based redditor canvassed the reddit community for members' impressions about MGM's Springfield project. The question elicited several detailed responses from Springfield-area residents who shared their perceptions about the proposed casino's location and feasibility, as well as its potential impact on local crime rates and employment. Even though such discussions are monitored by reddit community moderators, there is no guarantee that the statements I found were either accurate or based on fact.

Key Takeaways from Chapter Eight

- Social bookmarking websites help Internet users store and organize the destinations of their website visits.
- Page rankings on bookmarking websites are determined by algorithms that calculate the net number of community member upvotes and downvotes.
- Several reddit interest groups, known as subreddits, might be of interest to equity investors. Those interest groups include "Security Analysis," "Stock Market," and "Investing."
- Other useful bookmarking website resources include collections of tagged articles on Delicious and bulletin boards of users' pinned items on Pinterest.

CHAPTER NINE

Stocks Moving at Lightning Speed

Professional Traders Also Rely on Social Media

In earlier chapters of this book we looked at social media tools that can help you become a more informed stock market investor. Professional investors also try to decipher the information and trading signals embedded in the stock-related comments on Twitter and other social media websites. However, the deluge of raw, unfiltered data emanating from Twitter would be of little use to professional trading firms, without the role of intermediaries. They analyze tweets in an effort to separate fact-based comments from those comments based on rumor or misleading information.

In this chapter we'll examine the role of high-frequency trading (HFT) firms, as well as the function of the data science companies that act as intermediaries between social media websites and high-speed traders. We'll then consider the services provided by Dataminr (*www.dataminr.com*), an intermediary that analyzes Twitter messages to form an accurate picture of the present; as well as Gnip (*www.gnip.com*), which aggregates message streams from multiple social media websites and markets its distilled data to trading firms. Finally, we'll look at the services provided by other data analysis firms, such as Social Market Analytics, which assign sentiment scores to relevant tweets in order to help clients understand the implied mood of the stock market.

The institutional traders described in this chapter operate with technological and informational advantages over individual investors. For better or worse, the world of stock trading has always been dominated by powerful institutions. However, the best-informed individual investors *stay* informed by maintaining an awareness of the strides being made by professional trading organizations. Now that these institutions are taking full advantage of the market signals embedded in social media data, it has become more important than ever for you to develop at least a basic understanding of how these firms operate.

The Role of High-Frequency Traders

HFT firms rely on sophisticated computer algorithms to execute trades over very short time intervals—sometimes measured in microseconds. (A microsecond is *one-millionth* of a second.) HFT firms use computerized systems to initiate stock bids and offers with great rapidity. With infinitesimally small leads over other traders' orders, these bids and offers are able to make their way to the front of stock order queues.

HFT traders act with the certainty that there are "real" bids and offers—those from market participants other than HFT firms—elsewhere in the trading queue. If subsequent orders from other traders do not move in their favor, HFT firms can cancel their own orders. Alternatively, a high-frequency trader might be able to glean the apparent intention of other traders based on their order on one exchange, and then "race" them to another electronic exchange, where the HFT can act, based on this knowledge.

Given their ability to execute trades at unprecedented speed, HFT firms have been the subject of considerable controversy in the investment industry. They are also very powerful entities, having recently accounted for 50–70 percent of all stock market trading volume. As many as 90–95 percent of all stock quotes emanate from HFT firms. The discrepancy between the volume of HFT orders *placed* and the number of HFT orders *executed* suggests that many orders are being generated by traders who have no intention of carrying them out. In his March 2014 book, *Flash Boys: A Wall Street Revolt*, author Michael Lewis characterizes the phenomenon of orders being cancelled by HFT firms as "phantom orders." Readers seeking a more detailed account of the dynamics of HFT might consider reading *Flash Boys*, as well as Scott Patterson's 2012 book, *Dark Pools: The Rise of the Machine Traders and the Rigging of the U.S. Stock Market*.

For high-frequency traders, streams of social media data can be a powerful resource, as long as they have the ability to filter through the deluge of tweets and other messages, and quickly identify relevant messages that form an accurate picture of the current state of market sentiment. The ability to efficiently parse through huge volumes of social media data, and then to trade on it quickly and profitably, requires the related capacity to avoid all the "red herrings" out there: those Twitter messages that are based on unsubstantiated rumors or innuendo, or those that have been generated by individuals who might have reason to disseminate false or misleading information.

You might never work for a high-frequency trading firm or conduct trades using sophisticated trading algorithms. However, even with only an elemental understanding of how HFT firms operate, you can come to appreciate why such firms are well positioned to capitalize on the rapid stream of real-time information emanating from social media sources on the Internet. Individual investors should be aware of the role of high-frequency trading firms, as well as the technology companies that provide HFT firms with state-of-the-art social media data services.

Analyzing Social Media Messages: Some Basics

Learning about how technology firms and trading organizations use social media opens the door to some new terminology. While I endeavored to write this chapter with a minimum of "tech-speak," there are a few terms and definitions you should know so as to demystify what these technology and trading firms actually do.

The firms outlined in this chapter—Dataminr, Gnip, Social Market Analytics, iSENTIUM, and Eagle Alpha (*www .eaglealpha.com*)—form a bridge between social media websites such as Twitter and the trading firms that seek to gather intelligence from Twitter messages. As characterized by API Voice (*www.apivoice.com*), these analytics firms take in the "massive, real-time stream of tweets that flow from Twitter each day"—the so-called Twitter Firehose—clean them up, make sense out of them, and provide them to trading firms so that they can make decisions about stocks.

The cleaning up process involves a number of important steps. Duplicate messages are tossed out; the identity and location of Twitter message writers are verified; and the messages themselves are analyzed based on their use of language, words, and phrases. However, in order for firms like Gnip to scrub and analyze social media messages, their computer systems first have to be able to connect and communicate with Twitter, Facebook, and other social media outfits.

That is where Application Programming Interfaces (APIs) come into play. Gnip and other social data analytics firms purchase from Twitter the right to obtain access to Twitter's API. This API enables Twitter to deliver its message feed to website developers in a way that they can use. An API is a form of programming code that acts as a data conduit between two computing applications so that they can communicate with each other.

Key Terms to Understand

- *API (Application Programming Interface):* "An API dictates how two interfaces work with each other. In the case of social data, most information is shared through a *streaming API*."
- *Firehose:* "A term first coined by Twitter to describe their complete set of data. Now firehose, in conjunction with social media, means that [one] has access to the full set of a social media publisher's data."
- *Streaming API:* "With a Streaming API, [one's data] requests are ongoing, as is the data coming [one's] way after [one] makes the requests."

Source: Gnip Social Data Glossary (*www.gnip.com/resources/social-data-glossary*)

Dataminr: Analyzing Twitter Messages to "Predict the Present"

Founded in 2009, Dataminr is headquartered in New York City, on the outskirts of Manhattan's Silicon Alley. The company's mission is to identify "actionable opportunities when they first emerge in social media." By providing its clients with news alerts about business developments before they appear on mainstream media sources, Dataminr liberates investment firms from the onerous task of "manually monitoring . . . raw 'big data' streams." Dataminr undertakes this process by relying on its real-time access to the Twitter Firehose. The company customizes the "signal stream" it provides its financial clients based on specific investors' portfolios, sectors of coverage, and topics of interest.

Mark Dimont, Dataminr's former head of business development and finance, explained that Dataminr analyzes tweets in order to try to form a clear, real-time picture of news—essentially, a snapshot of what is happening "right now." Getting a clear read on the current status of events, and avoiding the pitfalls associated with acting on misleading tweets, is a process that Dataminr's CEO, Ted Bailey, refers to as "predicting the present."

NEGATIVITY AND SELECTION BIAS

In order to provide real-time updates for its clients, Dataminr must first ensure that its Twitter-sourced data is "scrubbed" to exclude the effects of several biases—what statisticians refer to as "negativity bias" and "selection bias." Negativity bias refers to the human brain's tendency to be more sensitive, and react more strongly, to negative news rather than to positive news. Selection bias refers to situations in which certain types of data are systemically excluded from a statistical analysis, resulting in a nonrandom data set that produces distorted results.

Dataminr's value to investors is that it helps identify news sources that are trustworthy, while flagging information that might be untrustworthy. Dataminr does this by analyzing the location from which Twitter messages emanate, the time that they originated, and the tweeter's social media influence as measured by a proprietary Dataminr system.

One notable instance of Dataminr's success in providing its clients with a timely news update occurred on November 5, 2013, when the company highlighted a tweet from Toronto's *Globe and Mail* newspaper. That tweet had indicated that BlackBerry was abandoning its search for a corporate buyer and replacing its CEO. While the original tweet had been transmitted at 8:12 A.M., mainstream media sources did not carry the news until 8:15 A.M. Dataminr's system notified the firm's clients of the corporate development three minutes before it was conveyed on newswire services, thereby enabling the company's clients to act quickly and sell shares in BlackBerry ahead of the curve. By 8:19 A.M. that day, the price of BlackBerry had fallen 20 percent.

Another instance occurred several months earlier. On March 8, 2013, Dataminr's clients received an alert that a Royal Caribbean Cruises Ltd. cruise ship had returned to its home port in Port Everglades, Florida, with 105 ill passengers who had contracted an illness caused by the norovirus. Dataminr's clients received that news update forty-eight minutes before it appeared on mainstream media venues, at which point Royal Caribbean Cruises's stock fell 2.9 percent. Having an early read on the news development enabled some Dataminr clients to adjust their positions in the stock before the news became widespread.

Gnip: Aggregating Data from Social Media Websites

Gnip was founded in Boulder, Colorado, in 2008. Gnip (pronounced *guh'nip*) derives its whimsical name from the word "ping," spelled backwards. Gnip provides a solution to the manner in which so-called "pull technology" functions. For example, many data companies have their servers transfer data to a customer only after that customer's systems initiate a request for an update. A customer's systems continuously "ping" the data publisher's servers, which increases the risk that the customer may end up receiving redundant data. Gnip tackles this issue by reversing the pinging process; Gnip customers either pull data from the Gnip servers or receive data that is pushed to them, at Gnip's initiative.

Gnip offers several services that are sourced from the firehose data emanating from Twitter and from other curated and crowdsourced financial websites, such as StockTwits and Estimize. Gnip's clients are not limited to the financial services sector; Gnip also provides its analytical services to advertising, retailing, education, and business intelligence organizations.

On April 15, 2014, Twitter announced that the company had acquired Gnip for an undisclosed sum. The acquisition underscores Twitter's recognition of the critical role played by data analytics intermediaries. Observers of the social media industry have begun to speculate about the implications of this acquisition for other technology companies that pay for access to the Twitter Firehose. Indeed, some of the data analysis firms profiled in this chapter now effectively compete against Twitter, the new corporate owner of Gnip.

Gnip Screens

Gnip subjects the raw data coming from social media sources to several screens. These systems gauge the message generators' use of language, their physical location, their Klout scores, and their embedded links and images. (As described by CrunchBase [*www.crunchbase.com*], Klout [*www.klout.com*] is a website that measures someone's online influence. This influence is based on how other Internet users engage with, and react to, that individual on social media websites and search engines.) Another Gnip offering, called PowerTrack, filters social media data based on the presence of certain keywords, links, and images.

Gnip also helps trading firms get access to the APIs of multiple social media websites. With Gnip, customers have a single source for accessing the APIs of many different social media services. The company also removes duplicate data and normalizes the format of the data from different social media websites. Other API sources aggregated by Gnip include Facebook, Flickr, Google+, Instagram (*www.instagram.com*), reddit, Delicious, and YouTube. Many of these social media websites are detailed in previous chapters of this book.

A related Gnip product enables customers to obtain access to the full historical database of public tweets since Twitter's inception. In November 2013, Gnip announced that it had further expanded its services and would begin to aggregate and make available the content of blogging and commenting platforms, such as Tumblr, WordPress, and Disqus.

To a layperson, Gnip's data services might appear similar to those offered by Dataminr. However, Gnip is classified by some technology industry practitioners as a social media "API aggregation tool" because of Gnip's ability to assimilate the data from multiple social media websites and to make that data available to its clients via a single API.

Social Market Analytics

Social Market Analytics (SMA) was founded in 2012. The company's operations are headquartered in suburban Chicago. Unlike Gnip, which aggregates data from multiple social media websites, SMA relies solely on Twitter's Firehose message feed for data. In some respects, SMA resembles other social media analytics firms discussed in this chapter. For example, SMA scrubs Twitter data in order to filter out spam, duplicate messages, and irrelevant tweets. According to the company's website, more than 90 percent of the tweets it analyzes are removed from consideration as candidates for inclusion in what SMA calls "indicative" tweets.

After funneling down its Twitter data to a group of indicative, or statistically relevant, tweets, SMA then computes what it calls "S-Scores," which are the company's proprietary gauge of stock market sentiment. For the statistically inclined, the S-Score sentiment index is defined by SMA as the "weighted normalized representation" of sentiment for a particular stock or index over a specified "look-back" period. Stocks with higher S-Scores have tended to outperform stock market indices, while those with lower S-Scores have tended to underperform the market.

SMA also provides several related statistics that help its clients gauge the direction and magnitude of changes in market sentiment. The company provides measures of "S-Volume," which is the volume of indicative tweets over a given timeframe. The company's "S-Mean" statistic measures the normalized, or "calm," sentiment state for a particular security or index. SMA clients can also look to related statistics such as "S-Delta," which is the percentage change in an S-Score over time; and "S-Volatility," which represents the variability of sentiment levels during a particular period.

Although SMA's services have been geared principally toward institutional investors, the firm recently began to market a subset of its sentiment scoring information to individual investors, who can purchase the data on a subscription basis. For monthly subscription rates ranging between $29 and $99, you can receive updated lists of the top ten and bottom ten stocks, as measured by SMA's S-scores, as well as watch lists of stocks and real-time alerts about high- and low-scoring securities.

SMA offers its subscribers access to its "Sentiment Score-board." The scoreboard features a graph of a stock's S-Score and

S-Mean—both calculated daily, before the stock market opens—compared to its closing stock price. The bottom of the scorecard tracks the stock's S-Volume and market trading volume.

iSENTIUM: Reading the Sentiment Signal

iSENTIUM (*www.isentium.com*) has offices in Montreal and Miami. The company uses the data supplied by the APIs of Twitter and DataSift (*www.datasift.com*), and analyzes the use of words and language in Twitter messages in order to gauge investors' sentiment about stocks. DataSift, a social data analytics firm, takes aggregate data from multiple social media websites, filters and analyzes the data, and then delivers it to clients. iSENTIUM is also able to use its technology to review analyst research reports by applying algorithms with linguistics capabilities.

In October 2013, iSENTIUM launched iSENSE, an app that tracks the market sentiment signals for 2,500 U.S. stocks. iSENSE is available as an application on the Bloomberg terminals found on most professional traders' desks. iSENTIUM clients are able to obtain access to the company's data stream, which interfaces directly with trading firms' algorithmic trading programs. Users of iSENSE can view a stock price chart with an overlay of sentiment indicators. This sentiment time series appears as a green line when sentiment is more bullish than average, and as a red line when sentiment is more bearish than average.

Gautham Sastri, iSENTIUM's CEO, explains that iSENTIUM does not envision its clients trading on the basis of current market sentiment but rather on the market signals *implied* by those measures of sentiment. This process involves anticipating the "mood" of stock market followers. Like other social media analytics firms, iSENTIUM subjects its data to certain adjustments, which are determined by the back-testing of data. Those adjustments might include the removal of certain large-capitalization stocks from indices in order to eliminate any statistical "noise" that would result from their inclusion.

iSENTIUM Case Studies

iSENTIUM's website features a series of case studies that illustrate the degree to which the trading prices of certain securities have followed the sentiment indicators generated by the iSENSE app. One case study cited by iSENTIUM involves the shares of Marvell Technology Group, a semiconductor company. On November 5, 2013, at 11:11 A.M., institutional traders using the iSENSE app on Bloomberg were alerted to a positive sentiment signal change for Marvell's stock. During the next nine minutes, Marvell's shares rose 7.5 percent. Between 11:15 A.M. and 12:00 P.M., mainstream news agencies began to report that KKR & Co., a private equity firm, had accumulated an approximate 5 percent stake in the semiconductor company. The stock of Marvell closed 8.6 percent higher during that day's trading session.

Another case study notes that on February 25, 2014, iSENTIUM clients were alerted to a positive sentiment signal change for the stock of Plug Power, a fuel cell technology company also mentioned in Chapter 5. Between February 25, 2014, and March 10, 2014, the shares of the company rose 64 percent, overshadowing a 1 percent increase in the NASDAQ Composite Index. On March 11, 2014, iSENTIUM's sentiment indicator for Plug Power turned negative. On that same day, the stock fell 41.5 percent after an analyst at Citron Research issued a negative report on the fuel cell company.

iSENTIUM's website highlights examples of the company's experience with gauging investor sentiment changes for ETFs that track commodity-based indices. iSENSE has followed the sentiment signal for the SPDR Gold Shares ETF, which turned positive in anticipation of an upward trading move in that security in July 2013. The app also predicted short-term directional moves in the United States Oil Fund ETF, which tracks the price movements of West Texas Intermediate oil.

Eagle Alpha: A Social Media "Dashboard Service"

Eagle Alpha was founded in 2012 by Emmett Kilduff, a former investment banker. The company is headquartered in Dublin, Ireland. Eagle Alpha's Social Sonar platform is a read-only service that enables subscribers to receive curated tweets, generated by approximately 15,000 preselected individuals, including business executives and government officials. One investment publication observed that Social Sonar resembles TweetDeck, one of the social media dashboard services discussed in Chapter 4.

Eagle Alpha selects the individuals it follows from the larger universe of tweeters based on their degree of online influence. The company then determines which tweets to forward to its subscribers, based on the input of both computerized algorithms and human curators. The company's founder describes Social Sonar as "a Twitter reader for financial market firms that . . . combine[s] technology with human input to get the best results." Social Sonar organizes influential tweets into lists, representing approximately 130 categories.

The basic, and least expensive, version of Eagle Alpha's Social Sonar costs $25 per month, or $240 per year. That service entitles subscribers to receive curated tweets from Eagle Alpha's universe of top stock market influencers. For $900 per year, you can subscribe to a more advanced version of Social Sonar, which offers customized lists for particular stocks or topics. A more expensive "pro" version of the software, which is marketed to financial services professionals, has additional capabilities. Because Social Sonar only retrieves incoming tweets without providing a mechanism for individuals to transmit messages, it conforms to the compliance requirements of many sell-side and buy-side financial firms.

Data Analytics Tools in Context

You can benefit by adopting at least some of the social media tools described in this book. You may choose to follow the tweets emanating from the investor relations offices of the firms in which you own stock, or use an RSS reader to peruse the blog posts of a few of your favorite journalists. Alternatively, you might open a StockTwits account and monitor the message streams related to one or two stocks in which you own large positions. However, monitoring your investments in this manner, without having at least some awareness of how big market players make use of this information, leaves you in a vacuum, isolated from, and oblivious to, the larger forces that might determine the fate of your investments.

Key Takeaways from Chapter Nine

- High-frequency trading firms, which rely on carefully screened social media data, recently accounted for 50 percent to 70 percent of all U.S. stock market trading volume.

• Technology firms such as Dataminr, Gnip, Social Market Analytics, and iSENTIUM purchase access to Twitter's Application Programming Interface. They then refine Twitter's data by eliminating duplicate and untrustworthy messages, analyzing linguistics, and vetting their senders' location and influence.

CHAPTER TEN

Social Media As a Tool for Investing Success

As the preceding chapters described, many of the aspects of social media can help you become a more informed stock market investor. And although social media applications can help you conduct financial and investment research, it is critical that you use social media to observe how other investors respond to company developments as they unfold. Such responses usually involve the coordinated use of multiple software applications. Twitter, investment blogs, RSS and newsreaders, as well as crowdsourcing and financial media websites, all play an important role in providing investors with an understanding of the context and impact of business events.

In this chapter we'll review two short case studies that explain how you can delve more deeply into the business events that sometimes precipitate material moves in stock prices. These examples will help you gain a better understanding of how you might use social media to assess these business forces. Finally, we'll close with several predictions about the future course of social media as an investing resource, as well as two examples of media and trading companies that are using social applications to tap into new audiences of investors.

"All Hands on Deck"

On Sunday, January 26, 2014, the day before Royal Caribbean Cruises Ltd.'s scheduled fourth-quarter 2013 earnings release, major media sources began to carry a story about a Royal Caribbean cruise ship that had suffered a major outbreak of a gastrointestinal illness. According to a statement issued that day by the U.S. Centers for Disease Control (CDC), 281 passengers and twenty-two crew members onboard the *Explorer of the Seas* had reported symptoms of the illness. The events prompted the cruise ship to return to its home port in Bayonne, New Jersey, two days before its scheduled arrival date.

Royal Caribbean was scheduled to report its earnings results before market trading hours commenced on January 27, 2014. In anticipation of the company's earnings release, as well as a possible adverse trading reaction to the prior day's reports of an outbreak of illness on the *Explorer of the Seas*, I began to monitor my Twitter and StockTwits accounts. At 5:30 A.M. I saw that StockTwits carried a message indicating that the consensus estimate for Royal Caribbean Cruises had stood at $0.18. My Twitter feed, prompted by a search under the cashtag "$RCL," revealed a series of messages, one of which cited an NBC News story indicating that the shipboard illness on the *Explorer of the Seas* had affected 600 passengers and crew members.

At 7:07 A.M. I received a *Seeking Alpha* news alert, confirming this number. By 7:58 A.M., Royal Caribbean's stock was down 2.3 percent in premarket trading from the previous day, as indicated on Yahoo! Finance. In preparation for the company's earnings announcement and any related social media message activity that might accompany it, I entered the cashtag symbol "$RCL" in my Hootsuite account. Subsequent premarket trading in the stock turned positive, with the shares quoted up about 1.6 percent by 8:20 A.M.

At 8:37 A.M. a message posted on StockTwits indicated that Royal Caribbean had just reported a fourth-quarter earnings-per-share result of $0.23, which exceeded the $0.18 consensus forecast. Almost immediately thereafter, my Hootsuite "$RCL" stream indicated that the stock was "ripping on earnings" and "up on earnings results." A subsequent message post on the Hootsuite stream confirmed that the company had beaten the consensus forecast by $0.05, but had missed quarterly expectations for revenues.

At 8:40 A.M. I received an e-mail from Royal Caribbean with the company's full earnings release, as well as a breaking news update from *Seeking Alpha* that confirmed the occurrence of a $0.05 earnings surprise. By 8:41 A.M. Royal Caribbean's stock was shown on Yahoo! Finance to be up 4.4 percent during the premarket trading session. Subsequent messages on Hootsuite echoed the news about the stock's strong premarket trading action.

While I had not yet had the opportunity to review the company's earnings release, a message on StockTwits, posted at 8:45 A.M., reported that the company had just announced 2014 earnings-per-share guidance of $3.20–$3.40. The low end of that earnings guidance range exceeded the then-current 2014 consensus estimate of $3.14. The favorable profit outlook helped explain why the stock was indicated to move higher in premarket trading. Several tweets on Hootsuite, posted a few minutes before 9:00 A.M., pointed out the strong related upward move in 2015 call options on the stock of Royal Caribbean.

After the Stock Market Opened

Shortly after the New York Stock Exchange's 9:30 A.M. trading opening, my Hootsuite dashboard, now updated to include a "$CCL" cashtag stream for Carnival Corporation's stock, revealed that Carnival, Royal Caribbean's largest competitor, was trading up 2.5 percent in sympathy with Royal Caribbean. By 9:42 A.M. Royal Caribbean's stock price, as indicated on Yahoo! Finance, had risen 3.6 percent in regular-session trading. After reading several tweets on Twitter about how investors were positioning their trades in Royal Caribbean's stock, I came across a useful message post on StockTwits. The message indicated that the company's strong fourth-quarter performance in Europe and Asia had offset the adverse effect of intense competition from other cruise line companies operating in the Caribbean.

While listening to the company's 11:00 A.M. earnings conference call webcast on my desktop computer, I noticed that Royal Caribbean's stock price gain had eased to a session advance of 0.7 percent, as reported on Yahoo! Finance. A 1 percent decline in the NASDAQ Composite Index revealed market-wide pressures on the performance of Royal Caribbean's stock. Despite a series of tweets that were focused on the recent incidence of illness on cruise ships, Royal Caribbean's stock subsequently recovered, with the shares quoted up about 2 percent by 1:30 P.M.

The foregoing case study provides a useful example of how you might use multiple social media applications, such as Twitter, StockTwits, Hootsuite, and webcasts, to understand the context of stock-moving events. The incidence of a cruise being cut short by a shipboard illness, right before the announcement of Royal Caribbean's quarterly earnings, created the potential for confusion among investors. Monitoring social media sources with the aid of online dashboard services can help you keep track of the market's reaction to rapidly developing news stories.

Walk Down the Aisle?

On Wednesday, January 29, 2014, a dramatic late-day trading move in the stock price of Isle of Capri Casinos, Inc., a small-capitalization gaming stock, provided another example of the immense value of using Twitter as an investment and trading research tool. On that day, the casino stock had risen 10 percent, with most of the major trading action having taken place between 3:21 P.M. and 4:00 P.M., the final thirty-nine minutes of the regular trading session. I first became aware of the spike in the stock's trading price when I received a *Seeking Alpha* news alert at 4:12 P.M. that afternoon. The *Seeking Alpha* e-mail indicated that "shares of ISLE put in some late volatility after several reports indicate[d] the company might be trying to sell itself."

Because the *Seeking Alpha* alert had cited a tweet from a gaming analyst at the research firm Hedgeye as its source, I immediately turned to my Twitter account, which revealed six recent tweets related to the late-day trading move in the stock. A Twitter message, posted at 3:27 P.M. by Hedgeye analyst Todd Jordan, indicated that "$ISLE may be up for sale reports say, but wouldn't be at much of a premium if any."

While that somewhat vague tweet neither revealed the original source of the speculation about the future of Isle of Capri nor confirmed its veracity, it did provide a starting point for explaining the stock's dramatic rally. I reviewed my StockTwits account, which revealed a message, posted at 3:33 P.M., indicating, "$ISLE is up for sale . . . or so goes the rumor." In order to obtain additional context for understanding the timeframe over which the rally in Isle of Capri's stock had occurred, I turned to the "Interactive Chart" facility on my Yahoo! Finance account and traced that day's minute-by-minute movements in the stock. The chart revealed the occurrence of several large trading moves and large trading volume spikes, which had taken place at 3:33 P.M., 3:45 P.M., 3:47 P.M., and 3:52 P.M. Even though the stock's price increased 14.4 percent during that thirty-nine-minute time interval, Yahoo! Finance neither conveyed any news stories about the trading surge nor identified its underlying causes.

Still trying to confirm the original source of the takeover speculation that had seemed to drive trading in the casino stock, I checked Isle of Capri's corporate investor relations website, as well as Yahoo! Finance's message board. Neither revealed any relevant news or information. In this instance, social media outlets such as Twitter were the only sources of commentary or insight that I could find on the subject. In order to continue to monitor business news and after-market trading action for Isle of Capri, I set up a cashtag-based search stream on Hootsuite using the symbol "$ISLE."

The late-day trading move in Isle of Capri on January 29 proved to be anticlimactic. No subsequent news emerged that either confirmed or denied the accuracy of earlier speculation that a sale of the company might be imminent. A subsequent tweet, posted on Hootsuite, dated February 1, raised the possibility of Isle of Capri's stock being a candidate for a short position, in the wake of the big run-up in its price. Another tweet questioned whether the stock had entered "overbought" technical territory. On February 3 a new tweet indicated that the stock had been downgraded by Thomson Reuters. I was not successful in identifying a proximate cause for the large trading move in Isle of Capri's shares on January 29. However, I would not have been aware of the speculative backdrop against which the move had occurred had I not been monitoring multiple social media sources for news updates and trading insights.

The Future of Social Media As an Investing Tool

Even though developments in the field of "social finance" have been well documented in business and technology magazines and blogs, the use of social media and financial tools is still in its nascent stage of growth. Many of the software applications described in this book are recent arrivals in the world of social media. Others will likely undergo a series of updates and refinements. The following paragraphs address what might lie ahead for social media, and its role in stock market investing.

1. *Improvements in Content Curation.* The technologies and processes that facilitate the curation of news stories, stock research reports, and trading commentary will likely continue to evolve and become more sophisticated. Popular techniques of content curation currently range from the manual retweeting of news stories and articles by blog writers, to the use of algorithmic programs that filter and prioritize the message streams on crowdsourced websites, such as StockTwits, and on news-reading applications, such as Flipboard and Paper. The array of curating tools currently available will need to be streamlined to make them accessible to a wider range of Internet users.

2. *Acceptance of Social Trading.* The recent commercial venture between StockTwits and Ditto Trade, which provides individuals with the ability to participate in the actual trades of more experienced investors, is likely a precursor of other developments in the field of crowd-based investing. Other firms, such as eToro, profiled later in this chapter, are aggressively pursuing capabilities that will enable investors to follow the leads of more seasoned traders. The pace of evolution of social trading will depend on the extent to which individuals trust the performance of social trading technology, as well as the leadership role demonstrated by well-known investors, whom some followers regard as trading mentors.

3. *Increased Penetration of Mobile Devices.* The channel shift from using desktop computing platforms to relying on mobile devices such as smartphones and tablets has been

a powerful trend, readily observable among consumers who use Internet-enabled devices. An increasing number of social media tools have been developed with the mobile user in mind. This shift in technology has been both a cause and a reflection of changes in consumer lifestyles, workplace design, and preferences. Whatever lies ahead for social finance, the important role of mobile Internet-connected devices is likely to be a critical one. As observed by social finance pioneers such as Howard Lindzon, the cofounder of StockTwits, social media applications will increasingly become a fixture within individuals' daily workflow.

4. *Embracing a "Second and Third Tape."* Howard Lindzon has referred to the growing acceptance of the existence of "two new tapes" as critical to the evolution of social finance. As described by Lindzon, the relevance of investment-related message streams emanating from Twitter and StockTwits will become more widely accepted. These two new tapes already coexist alongside the first tape—the electronic ticker-tape of stock trades that most of us are accustomed to seeing along the bottom of our television screens while watching CNBC. While a growing population of traders has embraced StockTwits and other social finance websites, it might take some time before the utility of these alternative online venues becomes widely accepted within the business and financial communities.

5. *Scrutiny of Blogger Credentials.* Several recent events have called attention to the problems that sometimes arise when bloggers and social finance community participants anonymously contribute written content. The blogging and financial analytics platform *Seeking Alpha* recently faced legal challenges and controversy as a result of its policy of permitting blog contributors to publish articles using pen

names. New safeguards might be needed to ensure that pseudonymous bloggers are free of conflicts of interest and are precluded from disclosing proprietary or confidential information about the subjects of their articles. It might also become imperative for blogging platform administrators to share information about their author vetting procedures, even as they continue to maintain the confidence of their contributors' identities.

The Controversy over *Seeking Alpha* Blog Articles

On February 14, 2014, Bloomberg reported that Greenlight Capital, the hedge fund run by noted investor David Einhorn, had sought a court order to compel the financial and blogging website *Seeking Alpha* to disclose the identity of a pseudonymous article contributor. That blogger reportedly disclosed the hedge fund's stake in Micron Technology before the information had been publicly reported. Einhorn claims that the blogger's comments about Micron Technology drove up the company's stock price, thereby increasing the cost at which his hedge fund had to purchase additional shares. On March 24, 2014, Bloomberg reported that Greenlight Capital had announced it was discontinuing its lawsuit against *Seeking Alpha*. Apparently, Greenlight Capital had successfully confirmed the identity of the pseudonymous blog writer without needing to pursue the lawsuit.

According to a February 2014 story in *Barron's*, *Seeking Alpha* removed from its website two articles that had expressed favorable views about the stock of Galena Biopharma, Inc. The articles about Galena Biopharma had been published under the assumed names of two different writers. However, it was later revealed that a single author had written both pieces. *TheStreet* linked the source of the two articles to a stock promotions firm that had been hired by Galena Biopharma.

Seeking Alpha is not the only blogging platform that permits its contributors to publish articles using pseudonyms. Some observers believe that allowing writers to express their views without revealing their identities allows for a degree of editorial candor that would not otherwise be possible. However, the presence of anonymous bloggers carries with it the potential for controversy.

Harvest Exchange:
The Future of Crowdsourced Research

Launched in December 2013, Harvest Exchange (*www.hvst.com*) was conceived by its founders to be a "network of friends, colleagues, and coworkers who were willing to share their thoughts and perspectives on the market." The website's professional membership includes notable hedge fund managers such as Kyle Bass and Daniel Loeb, each of whom has about 1,300 followers on the website. According to a profile article on Business Insider, visitors to the Harvest Exchange website are also "welcome to lurk, read, and consume the content."

On December 4, 2013, Bass, the founder and hedge fund manager of Hayman Capital, and an early-stage participant in Harvest Exchange, announced that his firm had taken a large investment stake in General Motors. Bass made his stake in the automotive company known via a presentation on Harvest Exchange. General Motors's stock rose about 3 percent in the immediate wake of media accounts of Hayman Capital's investment.

On January 21, 2014, the *New York Times* reported that Daniel Loeb, the founder of hedge fund Third Point LLC, had taken a major investment stake in Dow Chemical Company while urging that firm to spin off its petrochemicals business. Loeb had also chosen Harvest Exchange as the venue in which to publish a letter announcing his investment stake. The news of Loeb's involvement precipitated a 6.6 percent one-day rally in the shares of the chemicals manufacturer. Loeb's four-page report explaining the rationale for his equity stake in Dow Chemical Company can be retrieved by any Harvest Exchange member. Members can also see comments that other members have posted in response to Loeb's report.

The Harvest Exchange website offers many of the features associated with other social media websites discussed in this book. New members may join the website at no cost and can immediately begin to follow other investors, as they would on LinkedIn or Twitter. They may also invite their friends to join the website. In addition to reviewing comments and original research articles posted by other investors, Harvest Exchange members have the opportunity to manage a virtual portfolio, the investment returns of which are ranked against those of other Harvest Exchange members.

Visitors to Harvest Exchange can search for a company by its stock symbol and retrieve that company's stock chart and investment statistics, along with a chronological list of other members' message posts pertaining to that stock. While viewing another member's message posts about an investment, a visitor has the option of adding a comment or private note, or sharing the other member's comment with their own social media networks on Twitter, Facebook, or LinkedIn.

Upon joining Harvest Exchange, new members are allocated $1 million in "virtual" funds, which they can use to simulate stock trades. Members of Harvest Exchange are able to initiate hypothetical long or short positions in securities, as well as specify the percentage of their own virtual funds that they wish to allocate to certain stocks. Using virtual funds, members can also elect to "co-invest" with other members whose trades they might wish to emulate. By clicking the "+" icon on another member's message post, members can add the security cited in that original message to their own hypothetical investment portfolio.

Members can also search on the website for other individuals, including the highly regarded professional investors with which the Harvest Exchange website has become associated. Searching for an individual reveals that member's profile, including his firm affiliation, location, and recent message posts, as well as any previously posted reports that might help explain his investment positions. Member profiles also feature the number of other members who have elected to add virtual stock positions to their own portfolios based on the profiled member's stock recommendations, as well as information about the same-day and year-to-date returns that have been generated by the profiled member's hypothetical investments.

How Investors Use Harvest Exchange

Dennis Forst, a principal at Edgerton Advisors and a former sell-side equity research analyst, frequently turns to Harvest Exchange, as well as other social media websites, including *Seeking Alpha*, to augment his investment research on Bloomberg and mainstream media venues. Visiting these sites has made Forst aware of potential investment opportunities available in certain ETFs that offer the prospect of "broad industry participation" and a higher yield than might be available from individual equity securities.

According to Forst, social media websites have alerted him to "new ideas and food for thought" about investment topics that are not given much attention by mainstream media organizations. He also observes that traditional media outlets, such as CNBC and the *Wall Street Journal*, as well as their online affiliates, are too widely read by the investment public "to be of much value." Forst became more familiar with the broad range of information sources and ideas available on social media websites after a long career on Wall Street, where many financial professionals once relied exclusively on "mainstream" media channels.

eToro: The Future of Social Trading

In Chapter 5, we talked about the emergence of new financial platforms that facilitate crowd-based stock trading. StockTwits's agreement with Ditto Trade, an online broker, enables Stock-Twits members to "piggyback" on the purchases and sales of lead traders whose securities transactions they wish to emulate. Other financial firms have developed similar crowd-based trading platforms and allow clients the ability to copy the trades of other investors.

An Israeli online trading company called eToro (*www.etoro.com*) launched operations in 2007 with a platform that enables account holders to trade currencies and commodities. In 2012, the company launched an equities trading capability. While eToro's trading services are currently being marketed only to European customers and are not available in North America, eToro plans to expand its operations into new jurisdictions, where the practice of social trading holds promise.

In June 2011, eToro rolled out a feature called "CopyTrader" that enables its account holders to invest as much as 30 percent of their total account equity in the trades of a particular eToro member. Each account holder profile includes details about that individual's number of followers and "copiers," as well as his recent trading income and gains, open trades, profitable weeks, and a chart of his trading performances. eToro members have the ability to screen the company's member database in order to identify traders who have achieved certain performance benchmarks.

In May 2013, eToro reported that 64 percent of the trades recently executed on its platform had been copied trades. Those copied trades entailed an average position-holding period of thirteen days. eToro facilitates copied trades by enabling individuals to purchase "contracts for difference" (derivative instruments that mirror the movements of underlying securities), rather than to purchase the underlying securities themselves.

As is the case with many social media platforms, eToro has gained traction most quickly among younger audiences. According to the company's CEO, Yoni Assia, 80 percent of the current users of the eToro trading platform are in the 18–35 age range. Assia believes that a new generation of financial market participants is currently emerging. These younger individuals are more accustomed than their older counterparts to using social media in order to execute commercial transactions, including stock trades.

One of the business development challenges that Assia foresees in expanding the international footprint of eToro is that online trading has historically been a "locally fragmented" market, dominated by regional financial institutions. Assia believes that over time his company can develop a scalable international business model. Indeed, as more individual investors become familiar with StockTwits and other social finance applications, social trading is likely to become more widely accepted.

Conclusion

Harvest Exchange and eToro operate at the crossroads of finance, social media, and technology. Like the other crowdsourcing and microblogging websites discussed in this book, they are developing new platforms for investors to communicate and trade with each other. They have been joined by other technology firms that are endeavoring to redefine how business is conducted on Wall Street. One of these firms, Thinknum, has created a medium for analysts to automate, and collaborate on, the building of financial and valuation models.

While many of the innovations taking place in social finance have occurred in the institutional world of Wall Street, they are affecting individuals to an increasing extent. The message streams on Twitter and StockTwits, the blog posts on *Seeking Alpha*, and the discussion strings on reddit have the potential to alter the trajectory of market sentiment, as well as the performance of stocks owned by individuals. Investors should also bear in mind that many institutions who purchase data services from Dataminr and Gnip invest funds *on behalf of* individuals.

In the future, investors will witness the emergence of new media curation techniques and more sophisticated mobile trading platforms. The term "social media" is destined to become an anachronism that will be replaced by the more general term "media"—a catchall that describes the full range of communications tools available to people, as they engage in personal and business pursuits. It has never been more important for those with a stake in the financial markets to become familiar with the free online resources at their disposal. The applications and websites described in this book can be of great help in enabling you to develop a facility with these tools.

Key Takeaways from Chapter Ten

- Events involving Royal Caribbean Cruises and Isle of Capri Casinos demonstrate how social media resources can be used to link news events with stock trading moves.
- Advances in social finance may entail broader penetration of mobile devices, wider acceptance of social trading, and improved vetting of blogger credentials.

- Social media platforms such as Harvest Exchange have the potential to provide unique insights into the motivations and actions of activist investors.
- eToro, an online trading platform that uses "contracts for difference" to facilitate "copy-trading," has introduced innovations in the practice of social trading.

Social Finance Applications and Websites

Technology users have recently been inundated with new websites and applications. This is particularly true of the bookmarking website category of social media (discussed in Chapter 8).

Over time, the crowded field of social media apps may be thinned out by consolidation. Indeed, as this chapter was being written, the news-reading app company Flipboard announced that it had agreed to acquire a competing news-reading app platform, Zite, from its corporate parent, CNN, a cable news operation that is owned by Time Warner Inc. Until further consolidation takes place, social media website users will have to navigate a large and growing population of apps, many of which serve similar functions. The chapters of this book have been organized to facilitate the categorization of social media websites. However, even with the descriptions and practical examples provided in this book, you may find yourself overwhelmed by the sheer number of variations.

This Appendix includes a reference table that includes a list of sixty-three commonly used financial and social media websites and applications. For each application, you'll find the URL of the application's website and a brief description of its function and purpose. You will find it useful to refer to this table when you encounter an unfamiliar application or website or when you review earlier chapters of the book. Note that the contents of the table will certainly change over time, as new social media and financial websites emerge and others go by the wayside.

Guide to Social Media and Financial Websites and Applications

Destination	URL	Type of Application	Book Chapter
Benzinga	www.benzinga.com	News Aggregator	2
Bloomberg	www.bloomberg.com	Data/News	3
Business-week	www.businessweek.com	Data/News	4
CNBC.com	www.cnbc.com	Data/News	7
Covestor	www.covestor.com	Crowdsourc-ing	5
DailyFinance	www.dailyfinance.com	Data/News	6
Dataminr	www.dataminr.com	Data Analytics	9
Datasift	www.datasift.com	Data Analytics	9
Delicious	www.delicious.com	Bookmarking	8
Digg	www.digg.com	Bookmarking	8
Ditto Trade	www.dittotrade.com	Trading Platform	5
Eagle Alpha	www.eaglealpha.com	Data Analytics	9
Estimize	www.estimize.com	Crowdsourc-ing	5
ETF.com	www.etf.com	Advisory Firm	7
eToro	www.etoro.com	Trading Platform	10
Facebook	www.facebook.com	Social Network	4
Feedreader	www.feedreader.com	Newsreader	4
Felix Salmon's blog	www.felixsalmon.com	Blog	3
Flickr	www.flickr.com	Photo Sharing	8
Flipboard	www.flipboard.com	Newsreader	4
Financial Times	www.ft.com	Data/News	3
Forbes	www.forbes.com	Data/News	4

Gnip	www.gnip.com	Data Analytics	9
Google Finance	www.google.com/finance	Data/News	6
Google Hangouts	www.google.com/hangouts	Audio-Visual	7
Google+	www.plus.google.com	Social Network	4
Google Trends	www.google.com/trends	Search	6
Harvest Exchange	www.hvst.com	Crowdsourc-ing	10
Hedgeye	www.hedgeye.com	Advisory Firm	7
Hootsuite	www.hootsuite.com	Media Dashboard	4
Instagram	www.instagram.com	Photo Sharing	9
iSENTIUM	www.isentium.com	Data Analytics	9
iTunes	www.apple.com/itunes	Audio-Visual	7
LinkedIn	www.linkedin.com	Social Network	5
Market-Watch	www.marketwatch.com	Data/News	7
Minyanville	www.minyanville.com	Data/News	3
Morningstar	www.morningstar.com	Data/News	7
Newsify	www.newsify.co	Newsreader	4
Paper	www.facebook.com/paper	Newsreader	4
Pinterest	www.pinterest.com	Bookmarking	8
Pulse	www.pulse.me	Social Network, Blog	4
reddit	www.reddit.com	Bookmarking	8
Reuters	www.reuters.com	Data/News, Blog	3
Seeking Alpha	www.seekingalpha.com	Data/News, Blog	3
Shutterfly	www.shutterfly.com	Photo Sharing	8
Slate	www.slate.com	Data/News, Podcast	3

Social Market Analytics	www.socialmarketanalytics.com	Data Analytics	9
StockTwits	www.stocktwits.com	Crowdsourcing	5
StreetEYE	www.streeteye.com	Crowdsourcing	5
Stumble-Upon	www.stumbleupon.com	Bookmarking	8
SumZero	www.sumzero.com	Crowdsourcing	5
The Big Picture	www.ritholtz.com/blog	Blog	3
The Motley Fool	www.themotleyfool.com	Data/News, Blog	4
The Reformed Broker	www.thereformedbroker.com	Blog	3
TheStreet	www.thestreet.com	Data/News, Blog	3
TweetDeck	www.tweetdeck.com	Media Dashboard	4
Twitter	www.twitter.com	Microblogging	2
Vimeo	https://vimeo.com	Audio-Visual	8
Yahoo! Finance	www.finance.yahoo.com	Data/News	6
Yahoo! Voices	www.voices.yahoo.com	Crowdsourcing	3
YouTube	www.youtube.com	Audio-Visual	7
Zero Hedge	www.zerohedge.com	Blog	3
Zite	www.zite.com	Newsreader	4

Footnotes:

1. Flickr was acquired by Yahoo! Inc. in 2005.
2. Gnip was acquired by Twitter, Inc. in 2014.
3. Instagram was acquired by Facebook, Inc. in 2012.
4. Vimeo was acquired by IAC in 2006.
5. YouTube was acquired by Google Inc. in 2006.
6. Zite was acquired by Flipboard in 2014.
7. Delicious was acquired by Science Media Inc. in 2014.
8. Yahoo! Voices was shut down by Yahoo! in 2014.

Resources

The following books and articles were consulted in preparing this book.

Alcorn, Stan, "Twitter Can Predict the Stock Market, If You're Reading the Right Tweets," *Fast Company*, (*www.fastcoexist.com*), 25 April 2013.

Alden, William, "Startup That Analyzes Twitter for Wall Street Raises Financing," *dealbook.nytimes.com*, 27 February 2014.

Alternative Market Briefing, "Eagle Alpha Launches Social Sonar, a Compliance-Approved Twitterfeed," *www.opalesque.com*, 9 October 2013.

Asher, Jill, "Igniting Social Media: Technorati Interview with Jack Krawczyk, Senior Product Marketing Manager of StumbleUpon," *www.technorati.com*, 22 March 2012.

Bhasin, Kim, "Viral Photos Put Sears on the Defensive," *www.huffingtonpost.com*, 6 January 2014.

Bilton, Nick, *Hatching Twitter: A True Story of Money, Power, Friendship, and Betrayal*, New York: Portfolio Hardcover, 2013.

Bohn, Dieter, "Can Google Dominate Live Video with Hangouts on Air?" *theverge.com*, 29 October 2013.

Bollen, Johan; Mao, Huina; and Zeng, Xiaojun, "Twitter Mood Predicts the Stock Market," *Journal of Computational Science*, 2 February 2011, p.1.

Brown, Josh, "Can You Get Investment Knowledge from Twitter," *www.thereformedbroker.com*, 18 December 2013.

Browning, E.S., "Fun Fades at Investing Clubs," the *Wall Street Journal* (*online.wsj.com*), 3 February 2013.

"Brunswick Group 2014 Survey of Investment Community Finds 70% Believe Digital Media Will Play an Increasing Role in Future Investment Decisions," *Brunswick Group 2014 Survey of Investment Community* (*www.brunswickgroup.com*), 26 February 2014.

The Canadian Press, "Hootsuite Aims High as It Secures $165-million Funding Agreement to Expand," *Maclean's*, *www.macleans.ca/2013/08/01/hootsuite-aims-high-as-it-secures-165-million-funding-agreement-to-expand*, 1 August 2013.

Carr, David, "Left Alone by Its Owners, Reddit Soars," the *New York Times*, *www.nytimes.com*, 2 September 2012.

Chafkin, Max, "Kevin Rose Reigns as the Zen Master of Silicon Valley Chatter," *FastCompany.com* (*www.fastcompany.com/3004354/kevin-rose-reigns-zen-master-silicon-valley-chatter*), 15 January 2013.

Cheng, Jonathan, "US Stocks Recover from Fake Twitter Report, Power Higher," the *Wall Street Journal* (*online.wsj.com*), 23 April 2013.

Cheredar, Tom, "With Google+ Communities, Google Launches Its Own Version of Facebook Groups," *www.venturebeat.com*, 6 December 2012.

Chozick, Amy and Perlroth, Nicole, "Twitter Speaks, Markets Listen and Fears Rise," the *New York Times* (*www.nytimes.com*), 28 April 2013.

Constine, Josh, "Hands on with Facebook Paper," *www.techcrunch.com*, 4 February 2014.

Damouni, Nadia, "Winklesvoss Twins Invest in SumZero: Brothers Made Famous by Facebook Legal Fight Invest in Social Network," *Reuters* (*www.huffingtonpost.com*), 16 September 2012.

Drogen, Leigh, "Finance People Don't Have Pseudonyms, and Other Musings on Identity in Social Finance," *www.leighdrogen.com*, 19 December 2013.

Duggan, Maeve and Brenner, Joanna, "The Demographics of Social Media Users—2012," Pew Research Center (*www.pewinternet.org*), 14 February 2013.

Farzad, Roben, "A Guerrilla Stock Analyst Plays Mystery Shopper at Sears," *Bloomberg BusinessWeek* (*www.businessweek.com*), 30 January 2013.

Feuerstein, Adam, "Galena Biopharma Pays for Stock-Touting Campaign While Insiders Cash out Millions," *www.thestreet.com*, 12 February 2014.

Feuerstein, Adam, "*Seeking Alpha* Author Used Multiple Aliases to Tout Biotech Stocks," 28 January 2013.

Finger, Richard, "High Frequency Trading: Is It a Dark Force against Ordinary Human Traders and Investors?" *www.forbes.com*, 30 September 2013.

Fowler, Geoffrey, "Facebook Paper vs. Flipboard: Which App Delivers?" the *Wall Street Journal* (*online.wsj.com*), 4 February 2014.

Frommer, Dan, "eBay Dumps StumbleUpon," *www.businessinsider.com*, 13 April 2009.

Gilbertson, Scott, "Social Bookmarking Showdown," *www.wired.com*, 6 November 2006.

Globe Newswire, "Icahn Enterprises L.P. Issues Statement Regarding Twitter Account of Chairman Carl C. Icahn," *www.globenewswire.com*, 12 August 2013.

Goldstein, Matthew, "Hedge Fund Suit Seeks Identity of Anonymous Blogger," *dealbook.nytimes.com*, 18 February 2014.

Griffith, Erin, "Estimize Aims to Replace Sell-Side Analysts with Crowd-Sourced Earnings Estimates—and Now Gnip Is Selling Its Data," *www.pando.com*, 24 April 2013.

Ha, Anthony, "Social Data Startup Gnip Goes Deeper Into Twitter's Past, Offers Full Archive of Public Tweets," *www.techcrunch.com*, 19 September 2012.

Hagan, Joe, "The Dow Zero Insurgency," *New York Magazine* (*www.nymag.com*), 27 September 2009.

Harris, Derrick, "Startup Dataminr Claims It Gave Investors a Three-Minute Head-Start to Dump Blackberry Stock," *www.gigaom.com*, 4 November 2013.

Herbst-Bayliss, Svea, "'Loeb Effect' Buoys Social Media Site for Investors," *www.reuters.com*, 6 February 2014.

Holcomb, Jesse; Gottfried, Jeffrey; and Mitchell, Amy, "News Use Across Social Media Platforms," *PewResearch Journalism Project*, 14 November 2013.

Internet Week New York, "IWNY 2013 Panel: Financial Education for the Next Generation via Online and Social Media," *www.youtube.com/watch?v=ttzTzVP2nxY*, 29 August 2013.

Joyce, Sheryl, "Q4 Whitepaper: Public Company Use of Social Media for Investor Relations 2013; Part 1: Twitter and StockTwits," Q4 Web Systems, August 2013.

Kaye, Kate, "Buzz Beyond Facebook, Twitter: Gnip Pools Data from Tumblr, Wordpress: Combined Data Set Features Content from Popular Blog, Commenting Platforms," *Ad Age DataWorks* (*www.adage.com*), 26 November 2013.

Kerr, Dara, "Twitter Introduces Ticker Symbol 'Cashtags' for Finance Searches," *www.cnet.com*, 31 July 2012.

Kimelman, John, "When Investor Websites Get Duped," *Barron's* (*online.barrons.com*), 13 February 2014.

Klayman, Ben and Herbst-Bayliss, Svea, "Hedge Fund Hayman Capital Takes Stake in GM: Source," *www.reuters.com*, 4 December 2013.

Lagorio-Chafkin, Christine, "Introducing the Two Young Men Who Made Pinterest," *www.inc.com/30under30*, 2 July 2012.

Lardinois, Frederic, "There's Life in Delicious Yet," *www.techcrunch.com*, 6 October 2013.

Lardinois, Frederic, "Twitter Shuts Down TweetDeck for Android, iPhone and AIR, Discontinues TweetDeck's Facebook Integration," *www.techcrunch.com*, 4 March 2013.

LaRoche, Julia, "This Website Has Members Like Dan Loeb and Kyle Bass Posting Their Newest Stock Picks," *www.businessinsider.com*, 21 January 2014.

Lee, Edmund, "Associated Press Twitter Account Hacked in Market-Moving Attack," *www.bloomberg.com*, 24 April 2013.

Lewis, Michael, *Flash Boys: A Wall Street Revolt*, W.W. Norton & Company, Inc., 2014.

Lewis, Rob, "BrightKit Follower Sources New Hootsuite Name," *www.techvibes.com*, 9 February 2009.

Lopez, Linette, "Finance Pros Are Going Nuts over a New Database That Lets Them Compare Their Compensation Anonymously," *www.businessinsider.com*, 19 August 2013.

Loughlin, Chris and Harnisch, Erik, "The Viability of StockTwits and Google Trends to Predict the Stock Market," Spring 2013, *www.stocktwits.com/research/Viability-of-StockTwits-and-Google-Trends-Loughlin_Harnisch.pdf*.

Macmillan, Douglas, "New Reader App Zite Offers Olive Branch to Web Publishers," *www.bloomberg.com*, 4 April 2012.

Maheshwari, Sapna, "J.C. Penney Will Start Sharing Some Corporate News Exclusively on Twitter, and Some Analysts Don't Like It," *www.buzzfeed.com*, 16 January 2014.

Mauboussin, Michael, "Explaining the Wisdom of Crowds: Applying the Logic of Diversity," *Mauboussin on Strategy* (Legg Mason Capital Management), 20 March 2007.

Meyer, Robinson, "The Quiet Upheaval of Facebook's New iPhone App," the *Atlantic* (*www.theatlantic.com/technology*), 3 February 2014.

Miller, Zach, "Best Finance/Investing Podcasts on iTunes," *www.tradestreaming.com*, 7 February 2011.

Nappolini, Marco, "Social Finance: The New Influentials," *www.slideshare.net/MarcoNappolini1/social-finance-the-new-influentials*, 10 January 2011.

Nicholson, Chris, "Two Former CNBC Personalities Go to Yahoo! Finance," *dealbook.nytimes.com*, 16 March 2011.

Oliveira, Nuno; Cortez, Paulo; and Areal, Nelson, "On the Predictability of Stock Market Behavior Using StockTwits Sentiment and Posting Volume," *Progress in Artificial Intelligence: Lecture Notes in Computer Science*, Vol. 8154, 2013.

Patterson, Scott, *Dark Pools: The Rise of the Machine Traders and the Rigging of the U.S. Stock Market*, New York: Crown Business, 2012.

Pearlman, Phil, "It's Official, I'm Joining the Yahoo! Finance Team," *philpearlman.com*, 16 September 2013.

Pendola, Rocco, "More Pathetic Pictures from a Dying Sears, JCP (Update 3)," *www.thestreet.com*, 14 January 2014.

"RadiumOne Finds over 70 Percent of Consumers Favor Using Hashtags on Mobile Devices and Nearly Half Feel Motivated to Explore New Content When Hashtags Are Present," *www.radiumone.com*, 27 March 2013.

Roll, Richard, "What Every CEO Should Know about Scientific Progress in Financial Economics: What Is Known and What Remains to be Resolved," *Financial Management*, Vol. 23, No. 2, Summer 1994, p.69–75.

Roush, Chris, "Barron's Santoli Joins Yahoo! Finance," *Talking Biz News* (*www.talkbiznews.com*), 24 October 2012.

Saba, Jennifer, "News Reader Company Flipboard Buys Rival Zite from CNN," *www.reuters.com*, 5 March 2014.

Sabelhaus, John and Bogdan, Michael, "Appendices: Additional Figures for Equity and Bond Ownership in America, 2008," Investment Company Institute (ICI) and the Securities Industry and Financial Markets Association (SIFMA), 2008, p.87.

Salmon, Felix, "10 Reasons Barry Ritholtz Is Wrong about Gold," *Reuters* (*blogs.reuters.com/felix-salmon/2014/01/11/10-reasons-barry-ritholtz-is-wrong-about-gold/*), 11 January 2014.

Salmon, Felix, "The Definitive Twitter Value Play," *Reuters* (*blogs.reuters.com/felix-salmon/2013/11/07/the-definitive-twitter-value-play/*), 7 November 2013.

Schmerken, Ivy, "Estimize's Data Licensing Deal with Bloomberg Validates Social Finance," *Wall Street & Technology* (*www.wallstreetandtech.com*), 18 April 2013.

"SEC Says Social Media OK for Company Announcements if Investors Are Alerted," Securities and Exchange Commission, *www.sec.gov*, 2 April 2013.

Sharda, Dhiraj, "Yahoo! Finance Launches Market Pulse—a 'Real-Time' Stream of Information from the Web in One Place," *yahoofinance.tumblr.com*, 7 December 2010.

Subbaraman, Nidhi, "Dataminr Hooks Financial Firms on Speed," *Fast Company (www.fastcompany.com)*, 8 October 2012.

Summers, Nick, "Google Launches Hangouts, a New Unified, Cross-Platform Messaging Service for iOS, Android and Chrome," *thenextweb.com*, 15 May 2013.

Travlos, Darcy, "LinkedIn's Acquisition of Pulse Promotes Role of Game Changer," *www.forbes.com*, 15 April 2013.

Treynor, Jack L., "Market Efficiency and the Bean Jar Experiment," *Financial Analysts Journal*, May–June 1987.

Vlastelica, Ryan, "Twitter, Social Media Are Fertile Ground for Stock Hoaxes," *www.reuters.com*, 11 March 2013.

Walker, Joseph and Ante, Spencer E., "Once a Social Media Star, Digg Sells for $500,000," the *Wall Street Journal (online.wsj.com)*, 13 July 2012.

Wells, Georgia, "Tools Help Investors Wade through All the Chatter on Twitter," the *Wall Street Journal (online.wsj.com)*, 15 December 2013.

Whitcomb, Dan, "More than 300 Fall Ill on Royal Caribbean Ship; Cruise Cut Short," *Reuters (www.reuters.com)*, 26 January 2014.

Wilson, Sara, "Ben Silberman, Pinterest Founder and CEO, Talks Criticism, Fears," *www.huffingtonpost.com*, 27 November 2012.

Index